LAND THAT I L♥VE

Customize & Embroider Projects for Your State

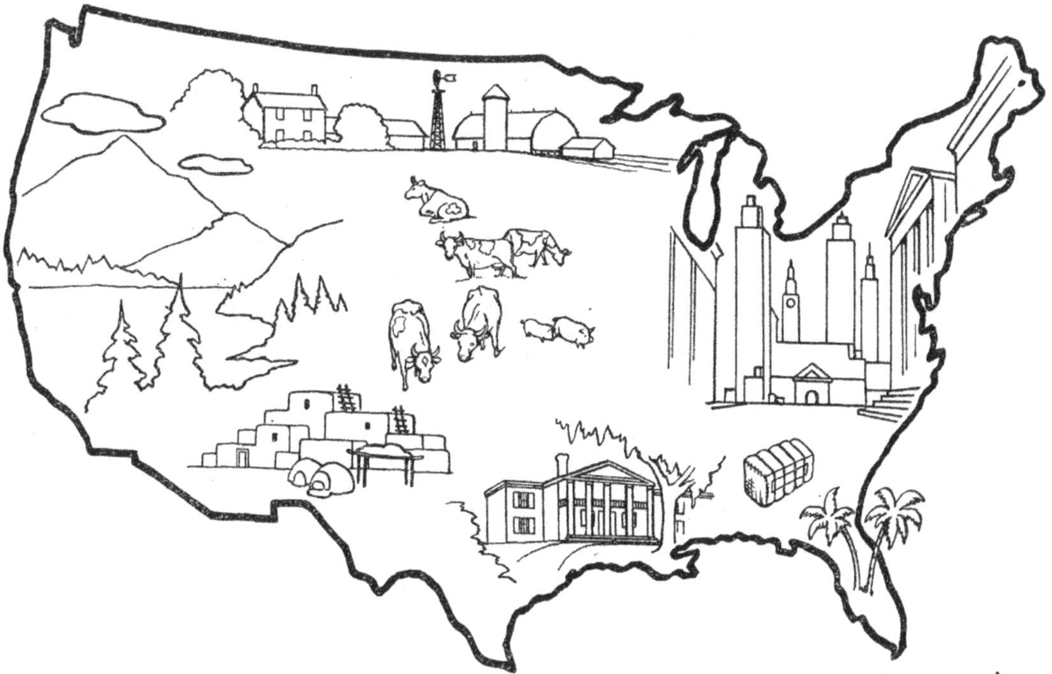

by Amy Barickman

All rights reserved, ©Amy Barickman, LLC. No part of this publication covered by the copyrights herein may be used in any form or reproduced for any commercial purposes, products or publications be it graphic, electronic or mechanical, without written consent of the publisher. Purchasing this book represents agreement that the buyer will use this book for personal use only. The purchaser may photocopy or reproduce the material to create custom embroidery designs for personal use only.

For wholesale ordering information contact Amy Barickman, LLC
at 913.341.5559 or amyb@amybarickman.com,
P.O. Box 30238, Kansas City, MO 64112

ACKNOWLEDGMENTS

A special thanks to the designers and production team who contributed to this book, especially Jan Durham, Robin Mackintosh, Grayson Price and Delsie Chambon.

Introduction

Land that I Love! Kansas has been my home for the last 25 years and that is why it is featured on the cover of this embroidery book. I am a proud graduate of the University of Kansas, where I received my degree in fine arts and design. I love being a Jayhawk alum and have a passion for KU's deep tradition in the game of basketball. (We won the National Championship when I was there in 1988!) After graduation, I founded my business, Indygo Junction, in Kansas City and now live in the suburb of Prairie Village. I am dedicated to bringing popular trends in the sewing industry to books, patterns, and needlework products. One such trend today is the love of home and wanting to share it, as well as the urge to roam or travel. When wanderlust strikes me—and it does every year—then travels take me and my family to the waters of Torch Lake, Michigan and the surrounding region. Sharing your roots and your region is a modern way to tell your story and feel connected to the community you love! Home Sweet Home!

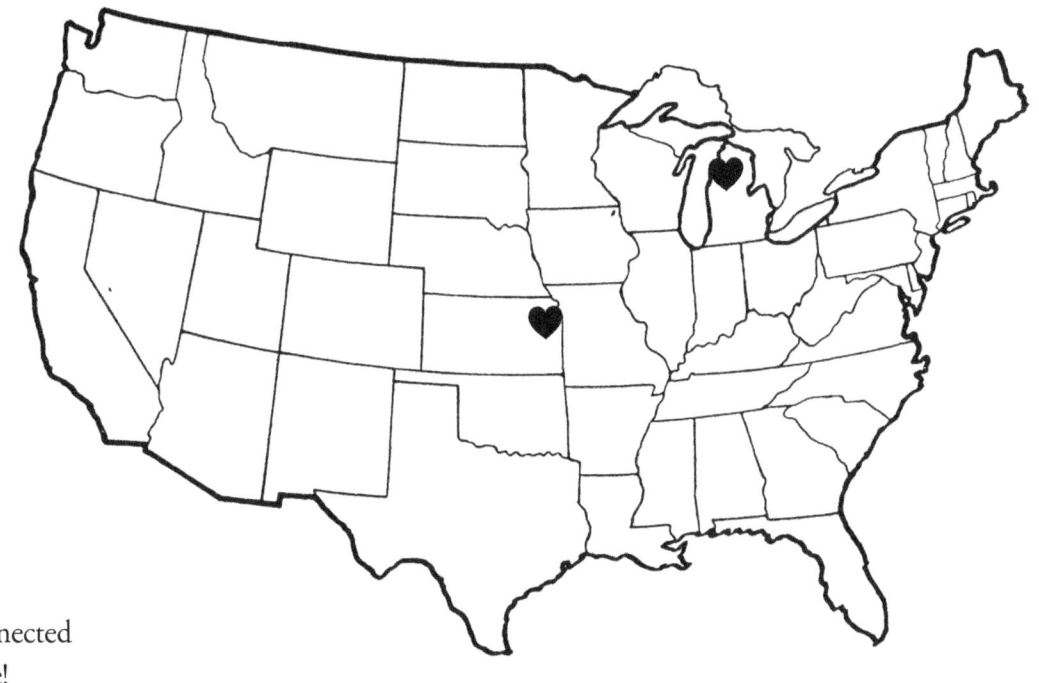

Vintage Made Modern… *Land That I Love* is another example of my passion for vintage design. I have been addicted to collecting vintage transfers for years, and the hunt for unique designs that have a modern flair is my passion. I have collected both finished quilts as well as many transfer patterns featuring state birds and flowers thinking creating a modern series would be a fun challenge. Here you will find the text and imagery to make your own personalized projects. We added lettering alphabets in the back of the book, so you can create your town's name or school if it is not listed. Keep in mind many motifs could be used for multiple states, so be sure to flip through the book to see all the possibilities!

The simple stitches of embroidery can provide the perfect way to express the wanderlust in your life. Whether your heart belongs to Texas, the wide open ranges of Utah, or the fields of California—in the pages of *Land that I Love*, you'll find the line art you need to create embroidered home décor that shows off your state pride.

My goal for this book is to provide embroidery makers with a very simple way to personalize their homes or make personal gifts for family and friends by using state pride as the focus. It is so easy, even for beginners, to make custom pillows or dish towels for any of the 50 states using the illustrations provided in this book.

The artwork on the following pages is designed for you to choose and use as you see fit. Our projects will provide inspiration for you to create and embroider your own one-of-a-kind stitchery projects. We encourage you to think beyond the ideas shown here. These designs can be framed for wall art or used on gifts for friends and family—there's no limit to what you can create.

And even if you have never embroidered before, no worries—we make it simple for you. The following illustrations are to scale for each of the 50 states:

★ the shape of the states in two styles and sizes

★ the state names in two font choices (and state's slogan)

★ state, flowers, birds, and major cities

★ university and college pennants

★ iconic motifs that distinguish that state's culture

For your own needlework, you can trace, transfer, or photocopy artwork right from the pages in this book. Our *General Instructions* will give you all the information you need along with tips and techniques to make your stitching experience a success!

You won't have to travel far from home when your creative skills can take you anywhere in the land that you love!

Enjoy,

Amy

P.S. We would love for you to share your creations online using #landthatIlove!

Starting Your Project

Creating your personalized state project is as easy as 1, 2, 3! We provide a vast library of motifs to pick from for each state as well as several alphabets that can be used to customize your project with names, dates, school or special location such as your hometown. To create your project, you will simply select your design, pick your favorite motifs, trace or transfer them onto your fabric and stitch!

Let's get started!

1. Pick your project. Use the instructions we've provided to create your own pillow or embellish a ready-made dish towel (we've included the details to create the towel we've featured on the cover). But don't stop there. There are many other ways you can use these designs. Try using them to create a quilt, embellish an apron to welcome a new neighbor, or keep it simple and display your project in a hoop or frame.

2. Pick your state or main design. Your project will need to start with a featured design that includes the motif. If you'd like to use a state outline, you have several options. Each set of pages comes with two options for the main state - a double outlined state that includes the state's name or a single outlined state featuring the state bird and flower. Each features a different font and can be reduced or enlarged as needed. The designs also provide space to add additional motifs. Note, the double outline state has been sized to fit on a dish towel for your convenience.

   If you prefer, you can use the state flower as your focal point as we did on the dish towel featured on the cover. Trace the flower off the single outlined state and select your favorite font style for the state name and flower.

3. Add the details! You can make your design as simple or complex as you want. On the back cover of this book, we show two double outline states, one features just a heart for Salt Lake City, Utah while the Ohio towel has a few additional motifs. Choose the details that tell your story - your school pennant, your hometown, your state flower, etc.

4. Trace, transfer & stitch. Now it's time to stitch. We've included all the basics that you will need to get started including: thread and fabric information, trace and transfer techniques, as well as basic stitch diagrams. Enjoy!

Threads, Needles & Fabric

In embroidery, as in life, the right tools will make your work a whole lot easier. Yes, you can embroider with just a needle and thread, but do you know what size needle and what kind of thread? What about hoops and scissors and transferring tools? There is a whole world of embroidery notions out there, and this guide will help you get started.

First things first. Thread. In this case however, we call it embroidery floss. There are a number of different kinds of embroidery floss and it can be somewhat confusing when faced with racks of it at your local store. For the projects in this book we used our Crossroads Decorative Thread from Sulky.

Threads

Crossroads Decorative Thread: 12 weight Crossroads Decorative thread from Sulky differs from traditional embroidery thread in that it comes on a spool. You may be surprised that you can embroider with thread on a spool but I find that I like working with spooled thread better than your typical embroidery floss.

When you work with spooled thread, you don't get all those messy tangles that inevitably come with embroidery floss. You can easily pull your thread off the spool to the length you desire. One strand of 12 weight thread equals approximately two strands of embroidery floss. You can add or subtract strands to get your optimal stitching line thickness. Crossroads thread is also extremely durable, which is great for the pillows & dish towels featured in this book.

Cotton Embroidery Floss: This is your classic go-to embroidery floss. The floss is made up of 6 strands of loosely twisted, slightly glossy thread. You will find this floss at all major craft stores, where you can buy the skeins individually or in color packs.

When using this floss you will often separate the threads from one another, depending how thick you want your stitching line. Typically 3 floss threads are used for stitching. However, if you want a thicker line in your design simply use more threads, if you want thinner, use two, however I don't recommend using one thread, it doesn't stand up to wear well.

Pearl Cotton: This cotton floss has a high sheen and comes in 5 weights (No. 3, 5, 8, 12, and 16) with 16 being the finest and 3 being the heaviest. Pearl cotton is 2-ply floss, so you don't separate the threads when stitching.

Other thread tips: If you will be creating a project that will be washed, check the colorfastness of your thread. It is important to use high quality thread such as DMC or Sulky to be sure your colors don't run.

When starting to stitch, keep your thread length to 15" to prevent tangles and knots while stitching.

Needles

You've picked out your project, you've picked out your thread, so now what? It's time to look at needles!

Embroidery needles, otherwise known as crewel needles, have sharp points with large, easily threaded eyes. Embroidery needles come in a variety of sizes, numbers 1-12, 1 being the largest, 12 the smallest. When choosing your needle size keep in mind that you want the thread to pass through the fabric with minimal abrasion, but the needle should not be so large that it leaves a noticeable hole around the thread.

Foundation Fabric

The fabric on which you work your embroidery is an important part of your design. Any fabric can be embellished with embroidery, here are just a few of our favorites.

Cotton or Quilting Weight Fabric: Quilting weight cotton fabrics are ideal for creating all different types of projects that can be embellished with embroidery, from purses and garments to home decor. Quilting weight cotton is easy to find in your favorite colors and patterns.

Blanks and Dish Towels: Another great way to jump start your embroidery is to embellish ready-made items such as aprons, pillowcases or dish towels. Companies such as Colonial Patterns create great "blank products" perfect for adding hand embroidery. If you'd like to create one of the five towel designs we've featured on the cover, we've included our choices of colors using our Crossroads Decorative Thread and the stitch diagrams for those designs to help you get started.

Crossroads Denim: Another ideal fabric is my Crossroads Denim line, which is a 54" 100% cotton denim weight fabric that comes in 19 colors. This is a great canvas for embroidery. The heavier weight of the material gives any project the sturdiness needed for heavy use. It makes it perfect for home décor projects and heavier weight garments like jackets or skirts.

Linen: Linen is a natural textile made from the fibers of the flax plant. Linen is a soft woven fabric, which comes in a variety of weights. Medium-weight linen is a great fabric choice as it has enough heft to hold the embroidery, but is light enough to use for garments.

Other Notions and Tips

A basic hoop consists of two rings, one that fits inside of the other. The larger, outside ring has a tightening device at the top to help keep the fabric taut. Hoops come in a myriad of different sizes and are made in either wood, plastic or metal. I prefer to use the wooden hoops. Hoop size will depend entirely how large a project you are working on and what you find most comfortable to hold.

Scissors are a must and I recommend getting specific embroidery scissors. They are smaller than a regular-sized pair, and those tiny shears are perfect for snipping the floss.

Thimbles are great for helping you push the needle through the fabric without poking yourself. They are worn on the index finger of your stitching hand, and protect your finger from those sharp points!

Needle pullers are rubber discs that help you pull needles through thick fabrics. If you are working with a heavier canvas, or a tightly stitched project, this will come in handy.

A needle threader is a nice gadget to have on hand. Sometimes it's tricky to get the needle threaded even when using a needle with a large eye. Needle threaders are very inexpensive and will take the frustration out of threading. The Clover Needlecraft brand is our favorite!

An iron is a must when sewing. Use one that has multiple heat settings for different fabrics, and a steam option. Note, when you are using an iron to transfer embroidery designs, turn off the steam.

A press cloth, or pressing cloth, is a thin piece of muslin or cotton that you use to protect your fabric, by placing it between your fabric and an iron. After you have finished your design and rinsed away the stabilizer if you chose that method to transfer, it is important to press out any wrinkles in your fabric. To do this, place a damp terry cloth towel on your ironing board, then lay your fabric right side down on the towel. Place a press cloth over your fabric and embroidery design. Use your iron to gently press out any wrinkles in the fabric. Do not press on the right side of the design, as that might flatten your stitching.

Transferring Embroidery Designs to Fabric

Now that you have your tools assembled, it's time to take the next step of transferring the project embroidery designs in this book to your fabric.

There are many methods you can employ to take advantage of the line art offered in this book. Each approach was used when creating the projects in this book. Experiment to see what your preferred method will be.

Wash-Away Stabilizer

One product that makes tracing and transferring embroidery designs easy is wash-away stabilizer. With this product, you are applying the design to the stabilizer which you then adhere to your foundation fabric. This helps keep your project pristine, as you are not applying any ink directly to your foundation fabric, and it helps protect your fabric while you stitch. This method also works well for darker color foundation fabric as stitching lines contrast against the translucent stabilizer.

Trace the design onto the stabilizer using any thin tipped pen. Following manufacturers instructions, adhere the stabilizer to the foundation fabric, hoop and stitch away. Use water to rinse away the stabilizer, again following manufacturers instructions, leaving only your stitched design. We recommend using Sulky's Sticky Fabri-Solvy or Sulky's Stick N' Stitch.

Keep in mind that the above products are sheets that can be fed through a printer, if you want to save time tracing the designs onto the stabilizer. To print the designs in this book, use an inkjet printer with a copier and set to "draft quality" to use the least amount of ink possible.

Iron-On Transfer Pencils + Pens

With this method you can turn any design into a heat transfer by tracing the design onto regular typing paper. Then, following manufacturer's instructions, you transfer the design to your fabric with an iron. These pencils and pens work with both lightweight and heavier-weight fabrics, however, they are permanent, so use carefully. They are also helpful to use to refresh iron-on transfer sheets you already have. A few of the products that we have used are: Sulky's Iron-on Transfer Pen Set, Collin's Iron-On Transfer Pencil, and Aunt Martha's Hot Iron Transfer Pencils.

Because the ironing process creates a mirror image of the design marked on the paper, be sure to trace the design in reverse on a lightweight sheet of paper. Make sure your transfer pencil is very sharp to keep the line as thin as possible so that it won't show outside of your embroidery.

Stitch Guide

The following pages show the basic stitches that we have featured in our projects, which are denoted with an asterisk. Experiment with the rest of the stitches to customize your design!

RUNNING STITCH*

SATIN STITCH*

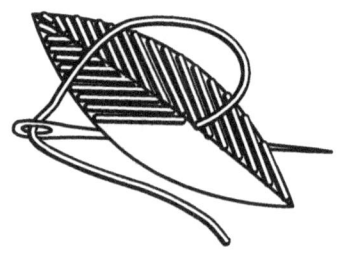

FRENCH KNOT*

LAZY DAISY*

BACK STITCH*

CHAIN STITCH*

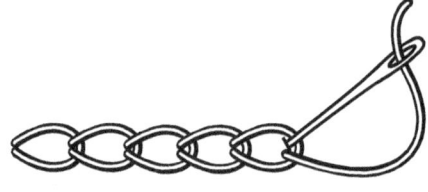

STEM STITCH*

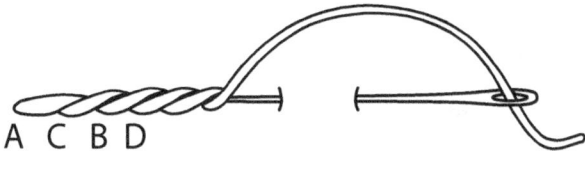

A C B D

FERN STITCH

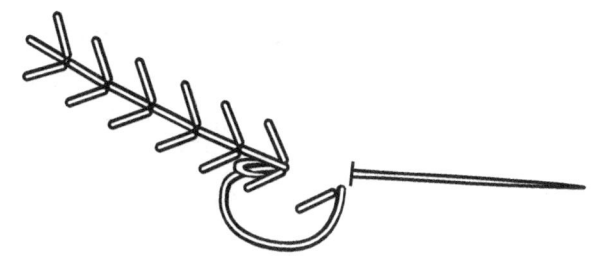

THREADED BACKSTITCH

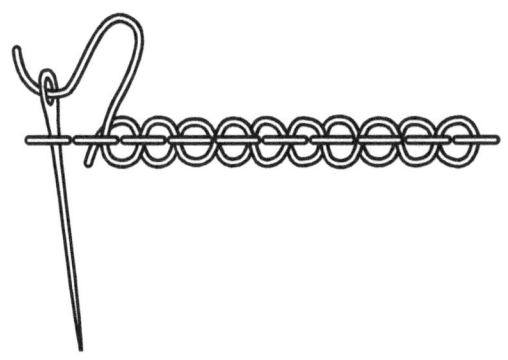

BLANKET STITCH

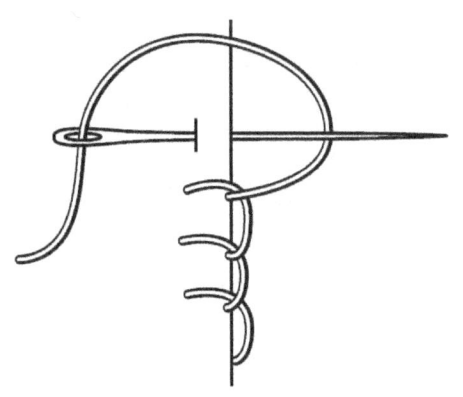

CHEVRON STITCH

DOUBLE CROSS STITCH

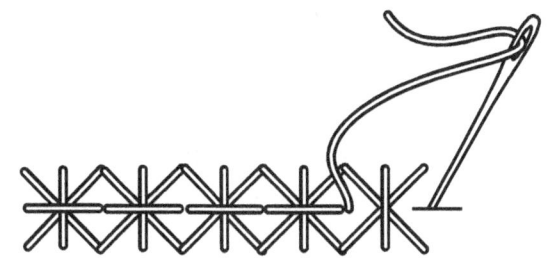

INTERLACED RUNNING STITCH

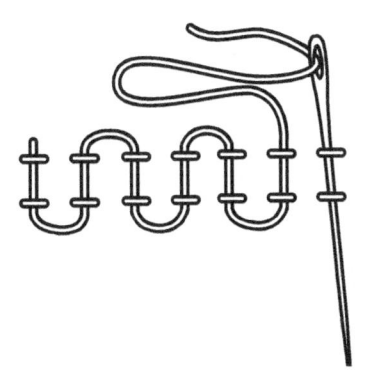

TIED CROSS STITCH

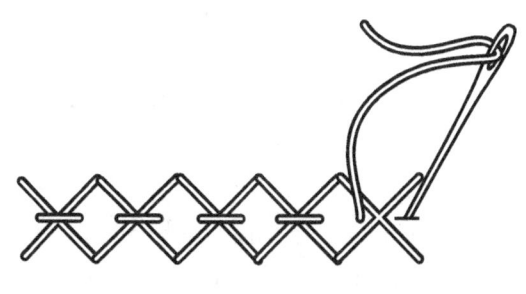

Land That I Love Projects

Below you will find instructions for creating the projects featured on the cover. We have included two pillow projects and instructions for stitching on finished dish towels. Keep in mind you can always add an embroidered state design to a ready made pillow, just appliqué it to the pillow top.

16" Ticking Pillow Instructions:
(pieced version, as seen on front cover)

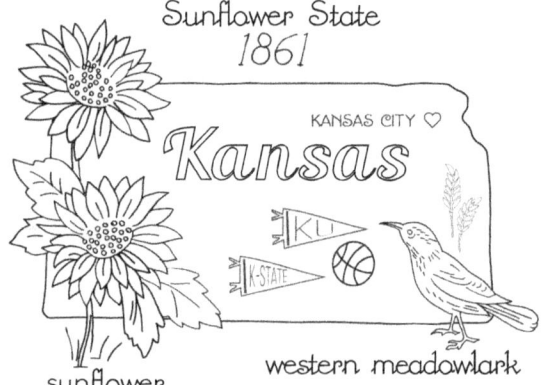

Cutting Instructions:
- Cut one embroidery backing piece 8 ¾" x 11"
- Cut two pillow top and bottom borders 5 ¼" x 17 ½"
- Cut two pillow top side borders 4" x 9 ¾"
- Cut two pillow back pieces 17" x 22"
- Cut 2" bias flange strips with remaining fabric.
Cut enough to create 2 yards of flange.

Assembly Instructions:
1. Using your preferred technique, transfer your embroidery design to the center of your embroidery backing piece. Stitch with your preferred stitches and thread colors.
2. When finished stitching your embroidery design, place back piece right sides together with one side border. Stitch with a ½" seam allowance. Repeat with other side. Press seam allowance open. The piece should now measure 9 ¾" x 17 ½". Place one pillow top border right side together to the raw edge of the embroidered piece, stitch. Repeat with remaining pillow top border piece. Press seam allowance open. Final piece will measure 17 ½" x 17 ½".
3. Sew together flange strips to make one 2 yard piece. Fold strip in half, wrong sides together and press flat.
4. Place raw edge of flange even with the raw edge of pillow top, cutting small slits to ease around corners. Corner may be rounded or squared off. Pin, Begin at bottom center, leaving 2" free at each end for attaching other end. Sew 3/8" seam all around. With right sides together, sew each end to the other at bottom center and continue the seam.
5. Fold one 22" side of pillow back pieces under ¼", press. Fold again ½". Press and stitch. Repeat with other pillow back piece.
6. Place remaining raw edges of each back piece to pillow top right sides together, overlapping the hemmed edges in the center. Pin. Stitch 3/8" seam, stitching over the previous seam line from attaching the flange.
7. Turn right side out and push out the corners. Insert 16 "pillow form.

16" Solid Pillow Instructions:
(as seen on back cover)

Cutting Instructions:
- Cut one pillow top 17" x 17"
- Cut two pillow back pieces 17" x 22"
- Cut 2" bias flange strips with remaining fabric. Cut enough to create 2 yards of flange

Assembly Instructions:
1. Using your preferred technique, transfer your embroidery design to the center of your pillow top piece. Stitch with your preferred stitches and thread colors.
2. To finish, follow steps 3-7 of 16" pieced ticking pillow instructions.

Stitched Dish Towels:

Use a ready-made finished dish towel as backing fabric for an easy stitch project.

Using your preferred technique, transfer your embroidery design to the center bottom of your dish towel. Test placement of design by folding and hanging towel as you wish it to be displayed. Stitch with your preferred stitches and thread colors.

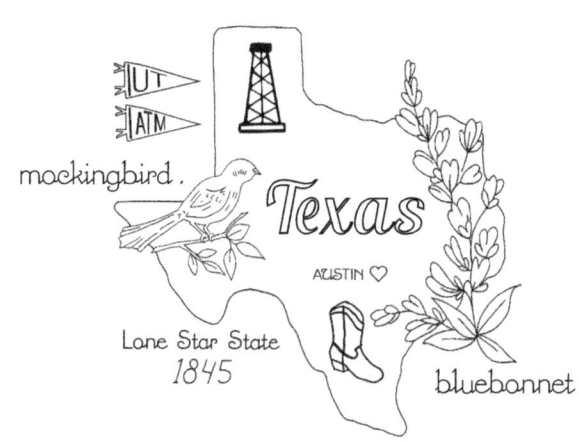

State Design Guide & Stitch Legend

Use this design guide for our suggestions for placing your own state's motifs! The following layouts, which are featured on the front and back covers, show how we have combined the different state outlines, flowers, icons, and name fonts for different projects.

Notice that we have listed recommended stitches for different elements of the design. Look at the Stitch Guide to learn how to create each stitch, then choose your preferred stitch. To create our recommended line weights, please read the tips below. Note, we used our *Crossroads Decorative Thread* on our projects. If you prefer using embroidery floss, note that one strand of Crossroads thread equals two strands of floss. Keep that in mind when recreating the line weight of the projects.

- The state title can be worked with a bold outline stitch for a fun, casual look. Work with four strands of Crossroads Decorative Thread and outline with a backstitch. For a classic or vintage look, work two or three strands and use satin stitch.
- When using the double outline motif, work with three strands of Crossroads thread in a tight chain stitch. Pairing this with a back or stem stitch in the inner line makes a nice contrast in texture.
- The single outline state motifs can be worked with three or four strands of Crossroads thread in a back, chain, or stem stitch.
- Small motifs, such as the pennants and other state icons, should be worked with two or three strands of Crossroads thread. Use one strand for the smallest details. Likewise, the number of strands for the bird and flower motifs should be scaled to the amount of detail desired, using two or three strands in most cases.

In order for you to be able to recreate the designs featured on the cover, we have also listed the color numbers of our Crossroads Decorative Thread that we used on each piece. When creating your own state design, use the colors of your choice.

Kansas Pillow Color Key

- **Sunflower:** petals (gold) #1024, center and veins (lighter brown) #0568, center dots (darker brown) #1058, leaves (green) #1176
- **Bird:** body (darker brown) #1058, chest (gold) #0567, feet (lighter brown) #0568, eye (black) #1234
- **Icons:** basketball (orange) #1246, KU letters (blue) #1253, KU pennant (red) #1039, K-State letters and pennant (purple) #1122, wheat (gold) #1024, wheat stem (lighter brown) #0568, heart (red) #1039, state outline #1180
- **Words:** Kansas, Kansas City, sunflower, western meadowlark and 1861 (black) #1234, Sunflower State (lighter brown) #0568

Texas Pillow Color Key

- **Bluebonnet:** petals (light blue) #1292, (blue) #1296, (white) #1001, leaves (green) #175
- **Bird:** body (black) #1005, (light gray) #1218, (dark gray) #1295 beak, eyes and feet (black) #1005, branch (light brown) #1180, leaves (green) #175
- **Icons:** boot (orange) #621, (light brown) #1056, (dark brown) #1130, UT pennant (orange) #621, ATM pennant (dark red) #35, Oil rig (black) #1005, heart (black) #1005, state outline (navy) #1199, (white) #1001, (red) #1147
- **Words:** Texas (red) #1147, mockingbird, Lone Star State, bluebonnet (navy) #1199, Austin (black) #1005

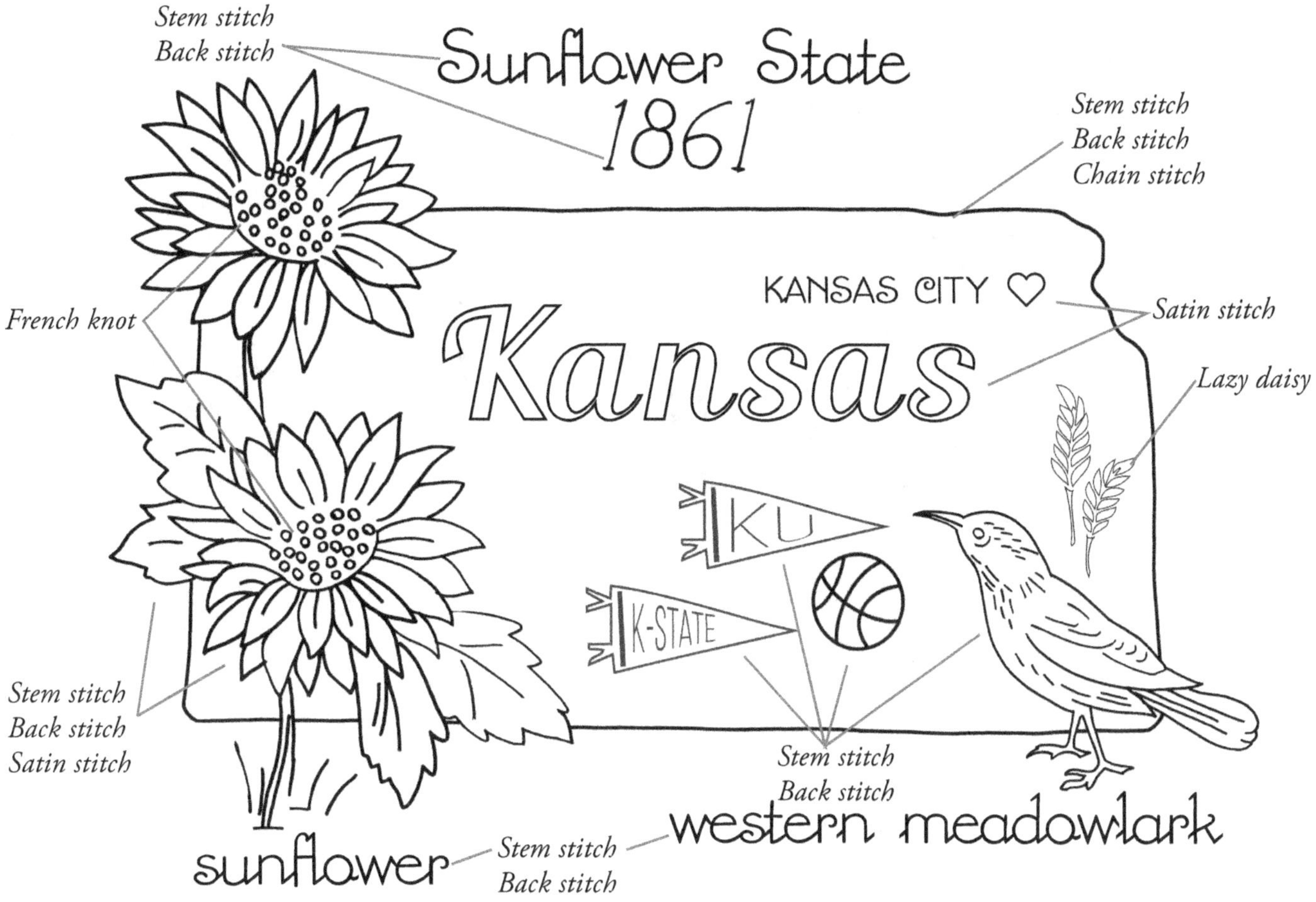

Texas sample with pennants placed outside of the state border.

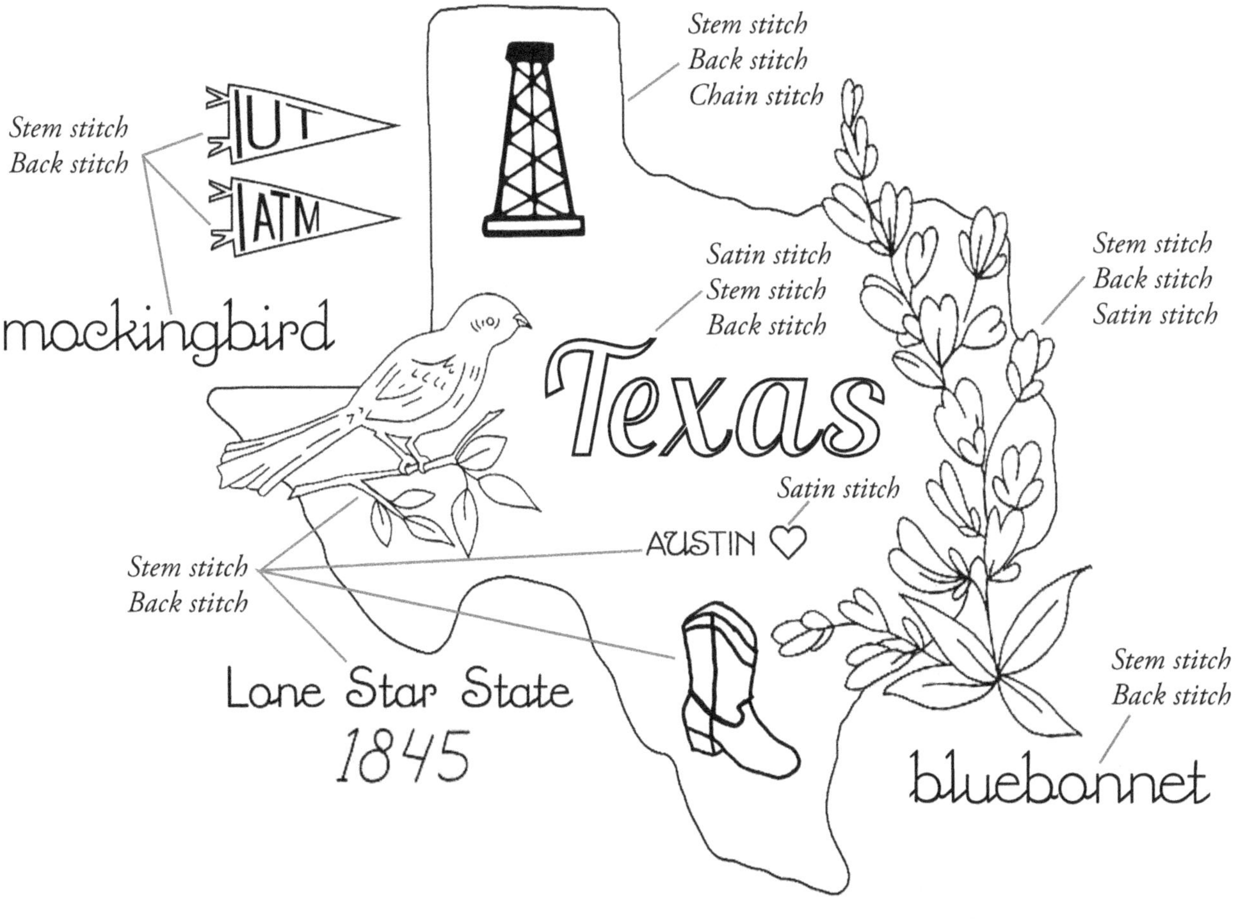

Towel Design Guide

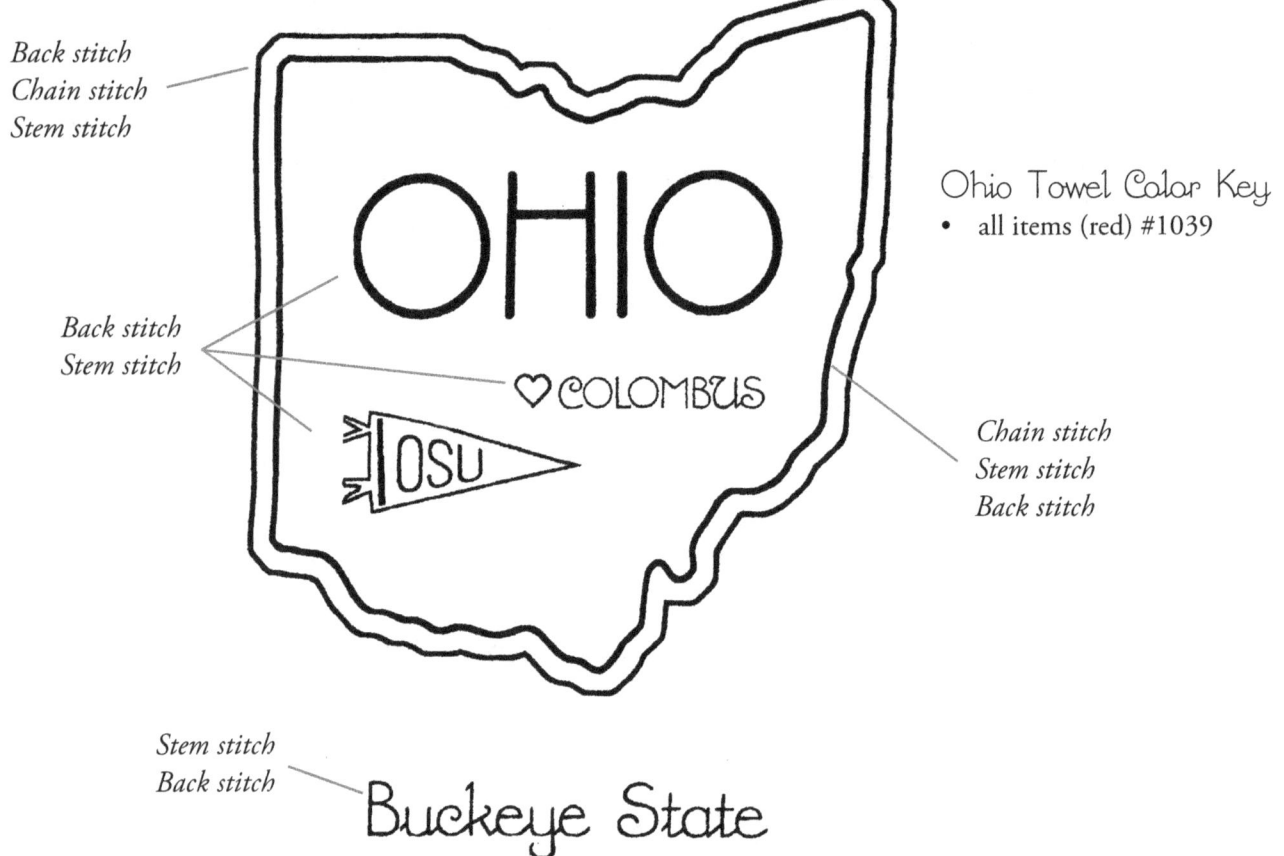

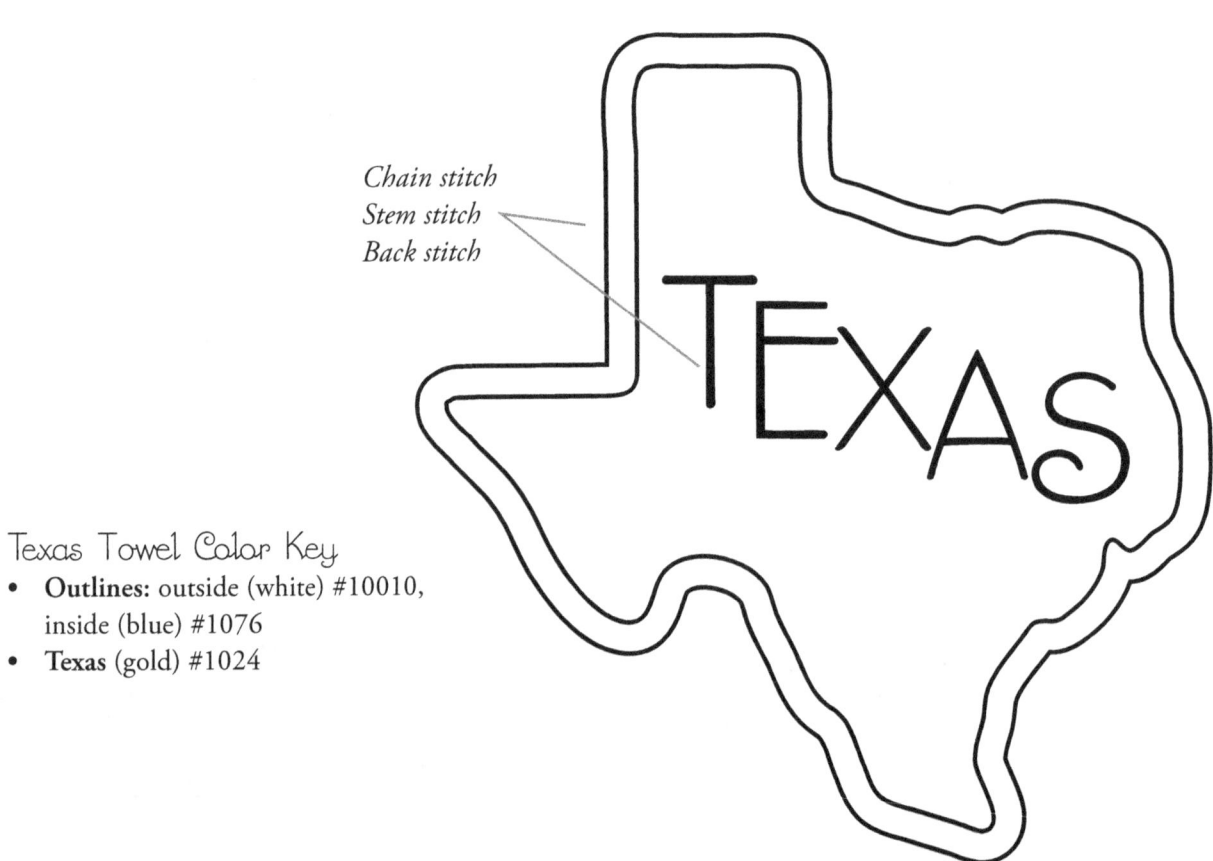

Texas Towel Color Key
- **Flower:** petals (blue) #1076, stem (green) #1825
- **Words:** Texas and bluebonnets (blue) #1076

Kansas Towel Color Key
- **Sunflower:** petals (gold) #1024,
  center and veins (lighter brown) #0568,
  center dots (darker brown) #1058,
  leaves (green) #1176
- **Words:** Kansas and sunflower (gold) #1058

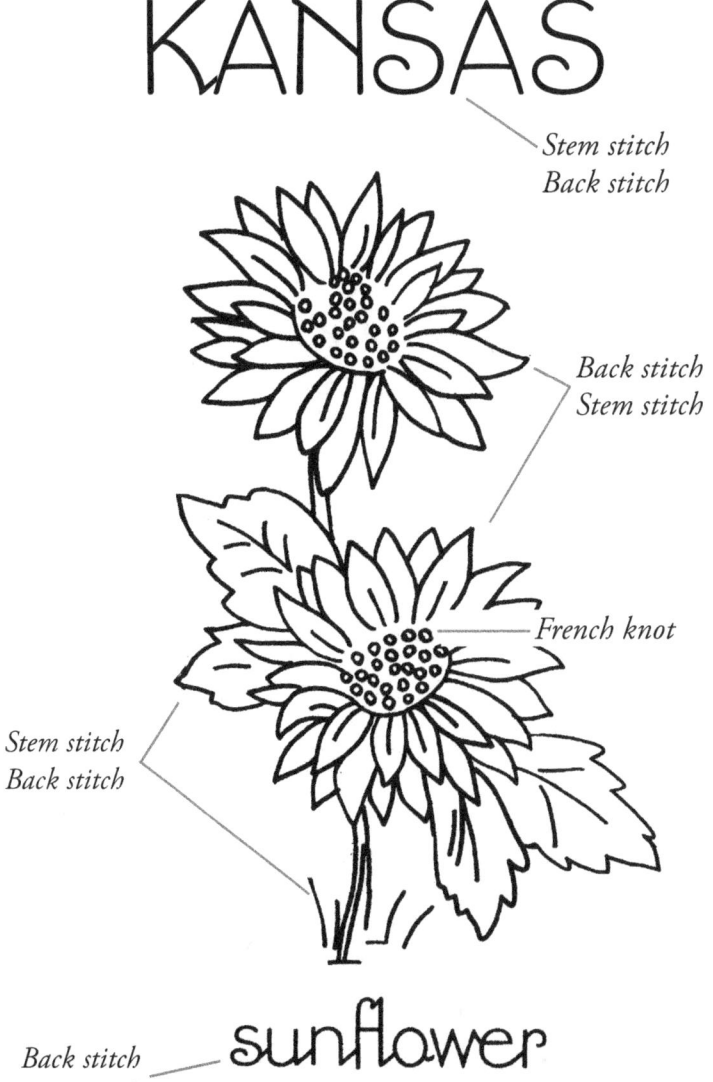

 # ALABAMA

Font Samples and Motifs

State Facts:

flicker
(state bird)

camelia
(state flower)

♡ ☆

Major Cities:

MONTGOMERY
BIRMINGHAM
MOBILE
HUNTSVILLE

Major Schools:

Auburn University
University of Alabama
Troy University

Towel Template:

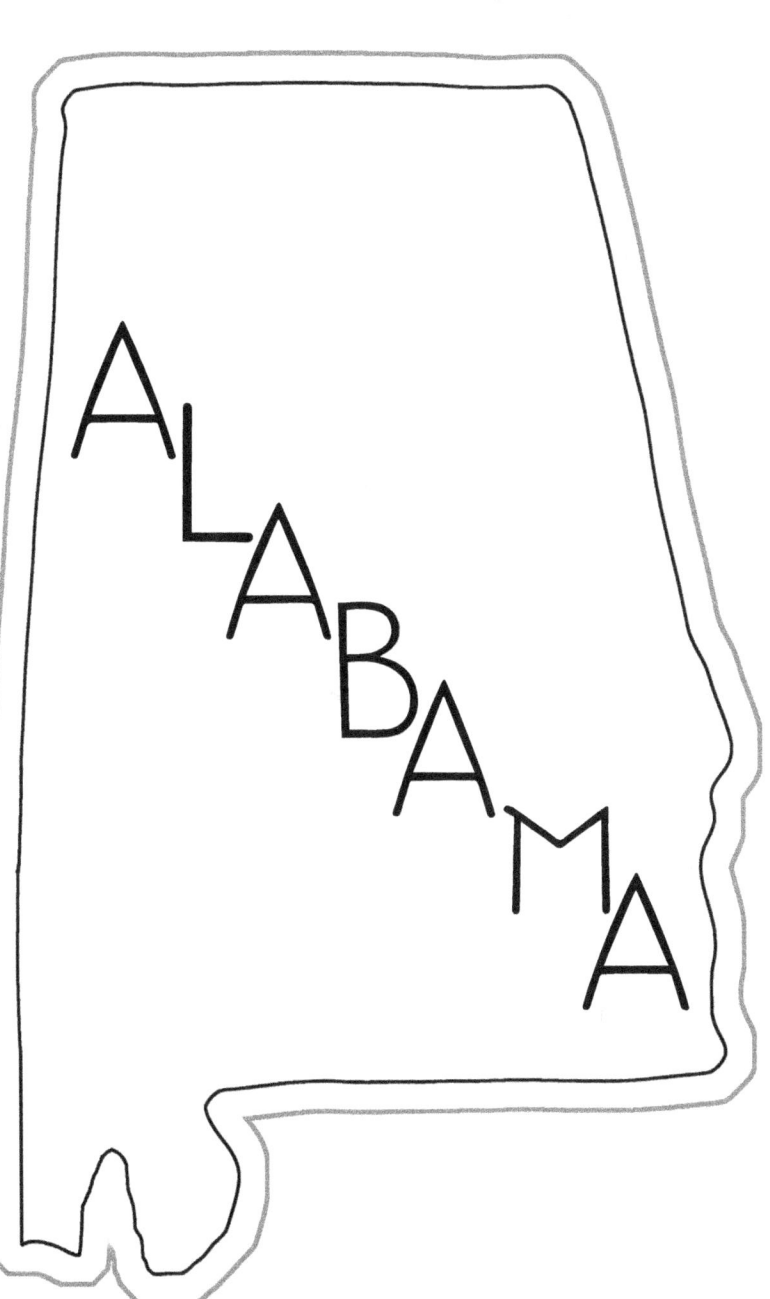

Iconic Marks:

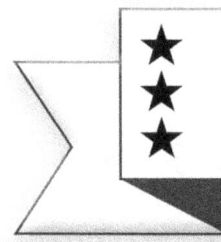 

ALASKA

Font Samples and Motifs

State Facts:

ptarmigan
(state bird)

for-get-me-not
(state flower)

Major Cities:

JUNEAU

ANCHORAGE

FAIRBANKS

Major Schools:

Alaska Pacific University
University of Alaska - Anchorage
University of Alaska - Fairbanks

Towel Template:

Iconic Marks:

 # ARIZONA

Font Samples and Motifs

State Facts:

cactus wren
(state bird)

saguaro cactus
(state flower)

♡ ☆

Major Schools:

Arizona State University
University of Arizona

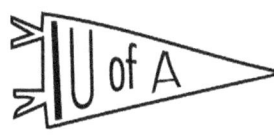

Iconic Marks:

Major Cities:

PHOENIX

TUCSON

MESA

Towel Template:

 # ARKANSAS

Font Samples and Motifs

State Facts:

mockingbird
(state bird)

apple blossom
(state flower)

Major Cities:

LITTLE ROCK

FORT SMITH

FAYETTEVILLE

Major Schools:

Arkansas State University
University of Arkansas

Iconic Marks:

Towel Template:

CALIFORNIA

Font Samples and Motifs

State Facts:

california quail
(state bird)

california poppy
(state flower)

Major Cities:

SACRAMENTO   OAKLAND
SAN FRANCISCO   SAN DIEGO
LOS ANGELES   HOLLYWOOD

Towel Template:

♡ ☆

Major Schools:

University of California – Berkley
University of Southern California
University of California – Los Angeles
Stanford University

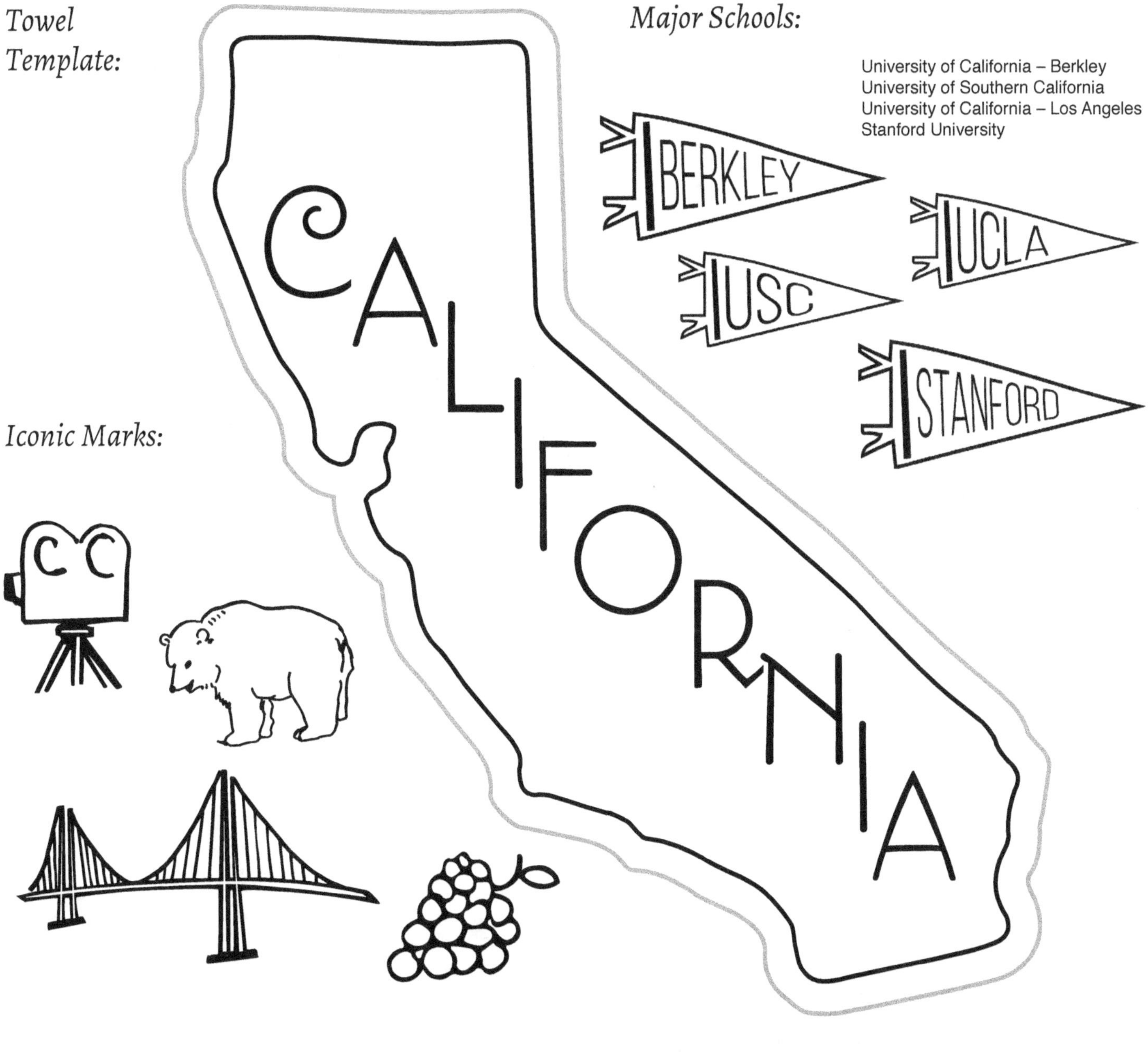

BERKLEY   UCLA   USC   STANFORD

Iconic Marks:

Colorado

Centennial State
1876

COLORADO

Font Samples and Motifs

State Facts:

lark bunting
(state bird)

columbine
(state flower)

♡ ☆

Major Cities:

DENVER
COLORADO SPRINGS
FORT COLLINS
GRAND JUNCTION

Major Schools:

Colorado State University
University of Denver
University of Colorado

Towel Template:

Iconic Marks:

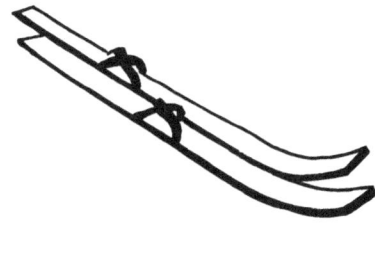

CONNECTICUT

Font Samples and Motifs

State Facts:

robin
(state bird)

mountain laurel
(state flower)

Major Cities:

HARTFORD
BRIDGEPORT
NEW HAVEN
STAMFORD

Major Schools:

University of Connecticut
Wesleyan University
Yale University

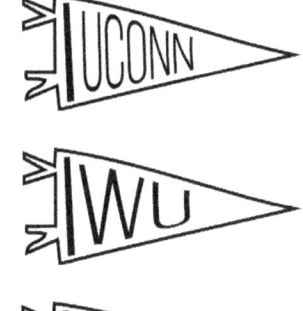

Towel Template:

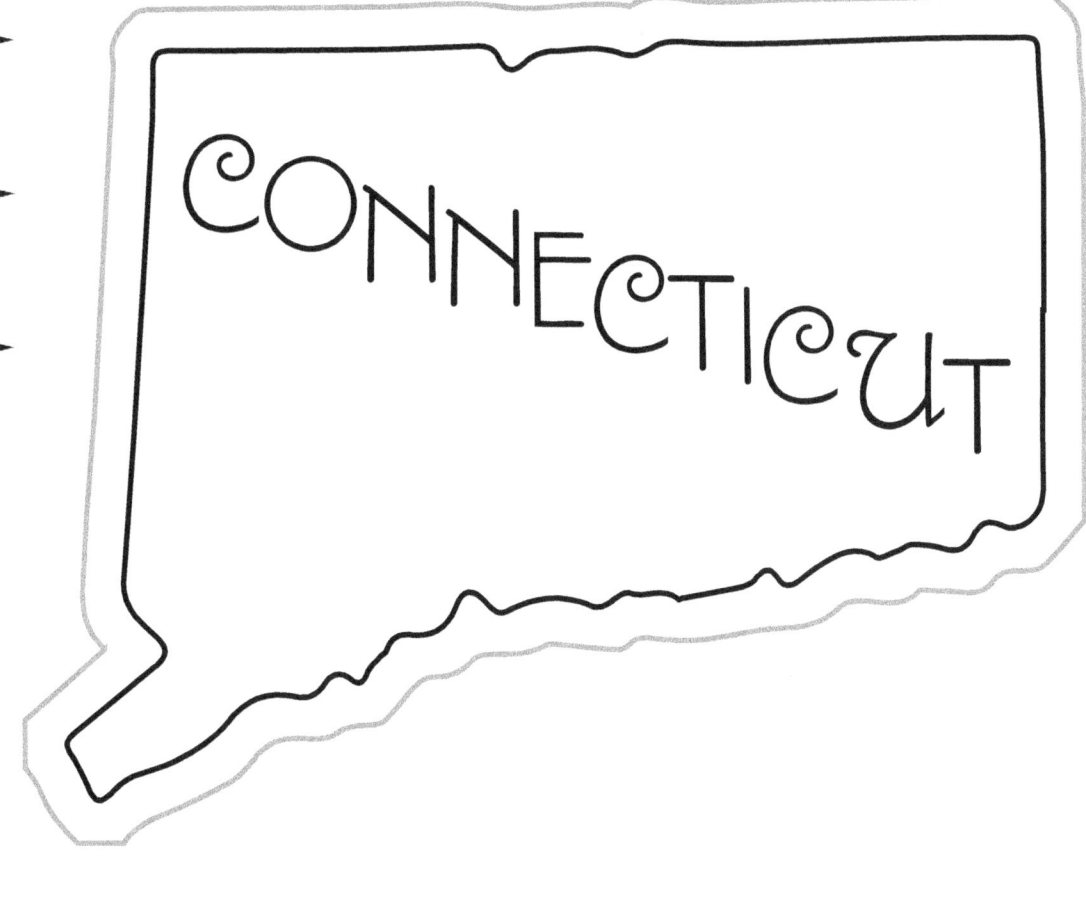

Iconic Marks:

First State
1787

Delaware

DELAWARE

Font Samples and Motifs

State Facts:

blue hen chicken
(state bird)

peach blossom
(state flower)

Major Cities:

DOVER

WILMINGTON

NEWARK

Major Schools:

Delaware State University
University of Delaware
Wilmington University

Towel Template:

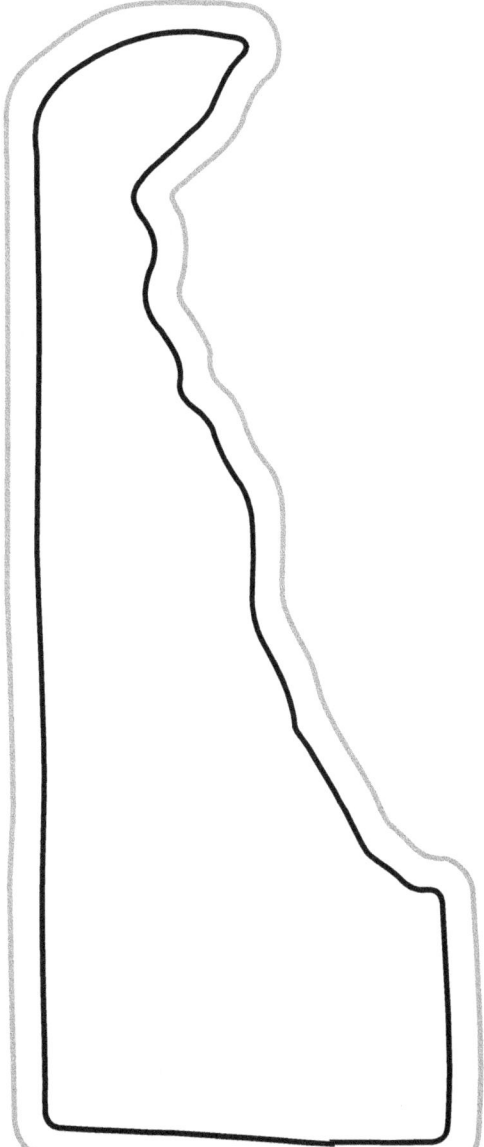

Iconic Marks:

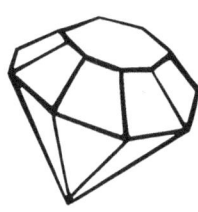

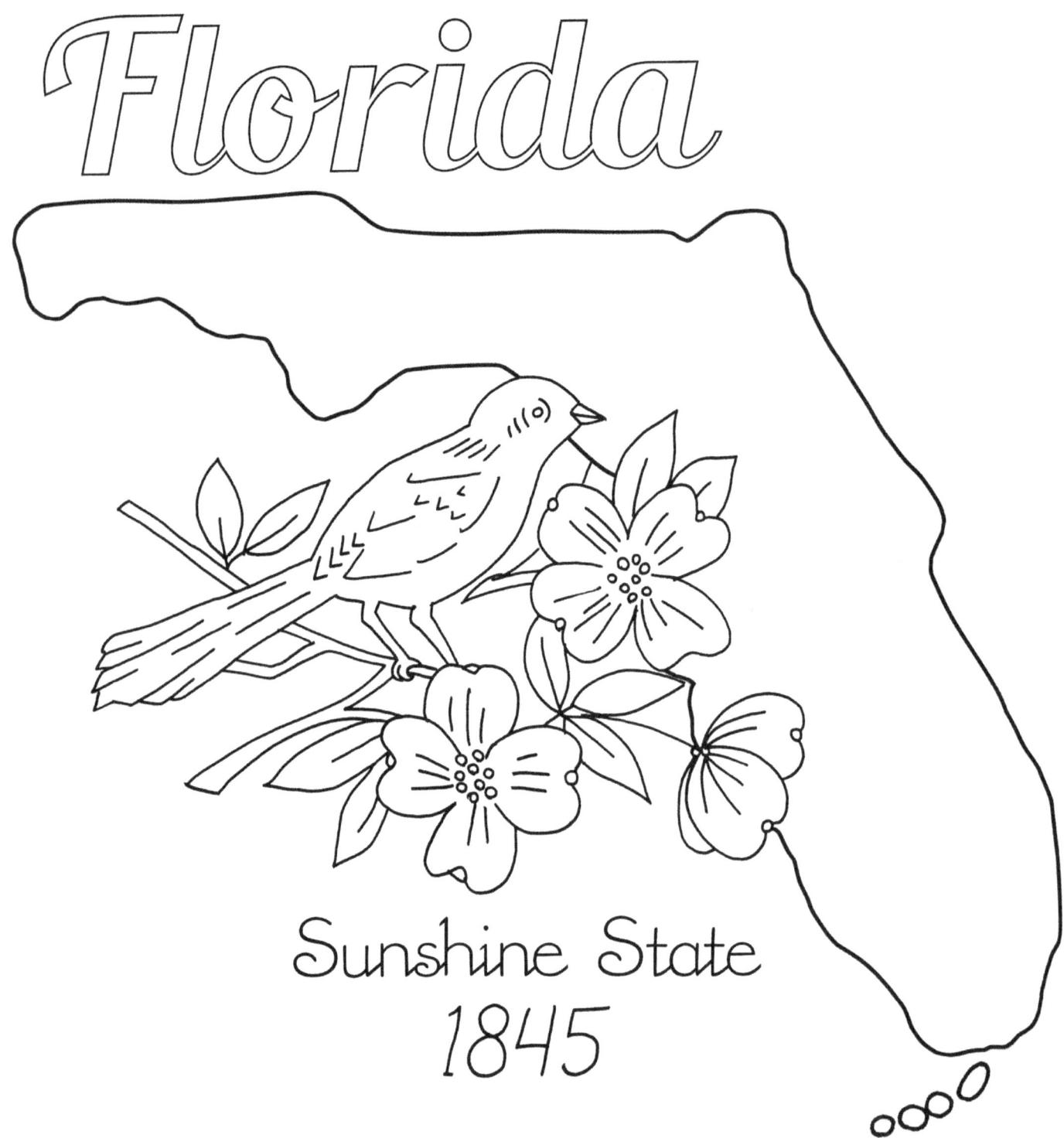

FLORIDA

Font Samples and Motifs

State Facts:

mockingbird
(state bird)

orange blossom
(state flower)

♡ ☆

Major Cities:

TALLAHASSEE   TAMPA

JACKSONVILLE   ORLANDO

MIAMI

Major Schools:

Florida State University
University of Florida
University of South Florida

Towel Template:

FLORIDA

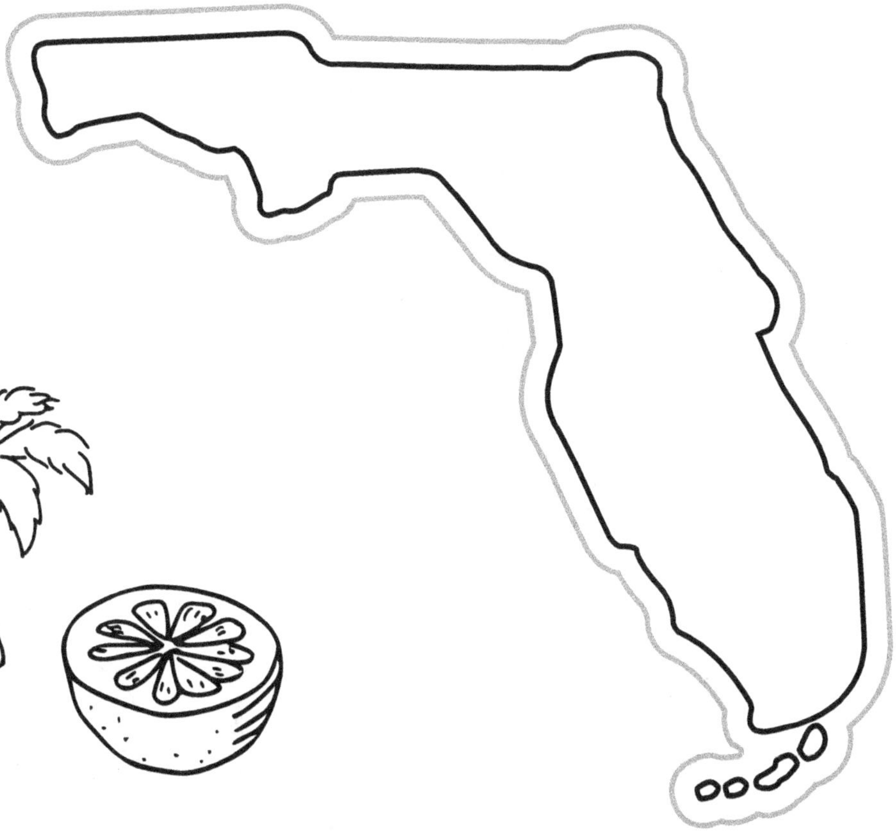

Iconic Marks:

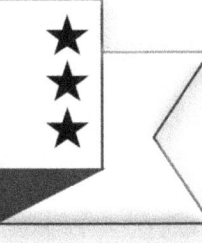

GEORGIA

Font Samples and Motifs

State Facts:

brown thrasher
(state bird)

cherokee rose
(state flower)

Major Cities:

ATLANTA

COLUMBUS

SAVANNAH

Major Schools:

Emory University
University of Georgia
Georgia Institute of Technology

Towel Template:

Iconic Marks:

HAWAII

Font Samples and Motifs

State Facts:

nene goose
(state bird)

hibiscus
(state flower)

Major Cities and Islands:

HONOLULU	KAUAI
HAWAII	MAUI
OAHU	MOLOKAI

Major Schools:

University of Hawaii
Hawaii Pacific University

Iconic Marks:

Towel Template:

IDAHO

Font Samples and Motifs

State Facts:

mountain bluebird
(state bird)

syringa
(state flower)

Major Cities:

BOISE
NAMPA
MERIDIAN
IDAHO FALLS

Major Schools:

Boise State University
Idaho State University
University of Idaho

Towel Template:

Iconic Marks:

ILLINOIS

Font Samples and Motifs

State Facts:

cardinal
(state bird)

native violet
(state flower)

Major Cities:

SPRINGFIELD   ROCKFORD

CHICAGO   JOLIET

AURORA

Major Schools:

DePaul University
University of Illinois
Northwestern University
University of Chicago

Towel Template:

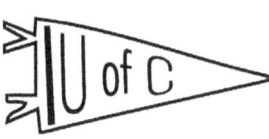

Iconic Marks:

INDIANA

Font Samples and Motifs

State Facts:

cardinal
(state bird)

peony
(state flower)

Major Cities:

INDIANAPOLIS
FORT WAYNE
EVANSVILLE
SOUTH BEND

Major Schools:

Ball State University
Notre Dame University
Indiana University
Purdue University

Towel Template:

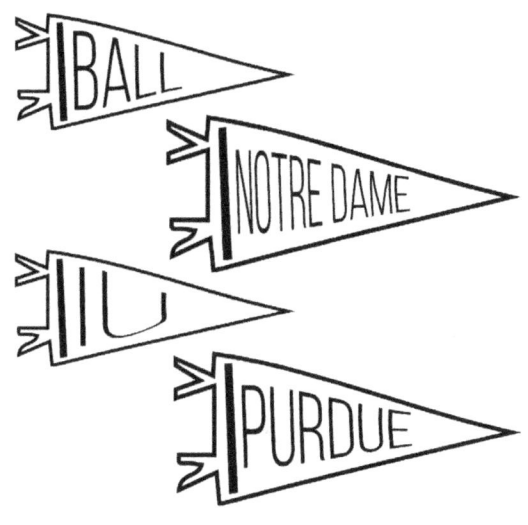

Iconic Marks:

IOWA

Font Samples and Motifs

State Facts:

goldfinch
(state bird)

wild rose
(state flower)

Major Cities:

IOWA CITY
DES MOINES
CEDAR RAPIDS
DAVENPORT

Major Schools:

Iowa State
University of Iowa
University of Northern Iowa

Towel Template:

Iconic Marks:

KANSAS

Font Samples and Motifs

State Facts:

western meadowlark
(state bird)

sunflower
(state flower)

Major Cities:

TOPEKA
WICHITA
KANSAS CITY
LAWRENCE

Major Schools:

University of Kansas
Kansas State University
Wichita State University

Iconic Marks:

Towel Template:

KENTUCKY

Font Samples and Motifs

State Facts:

cardinal
(state bird)

goldenrod
(state flower)

Major Cities:

FRANKFURT

LEXINGTON

LOUISVILLE

Major Schools:

University of Kentucky
University of Louisville

Iconic Marks:

Towel Template:

KENTUCKY

LOUISIANA

Font Samples and Motifs

State Facts:

brown pelican
(state bird)

magnolia
(state flower)

♡ ☆

Major Cities:

BATON ROUGE
NEW ORLEANS
SHREVEPORT
LAFAYETTE

Major Schools:

Louisiana State University
Tulane University

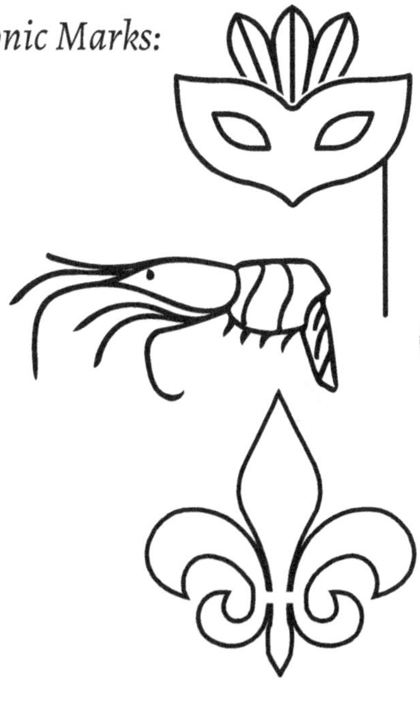

Towel Template:

Iconic Marks:

MAINE

Font Samples and Motifs

State Facts:

black-capped chickadee
(state bird)

pine cone and tassel
(state flower)

Major Cities:

AUGUSTA
PORTLAND
LEWISTON
BANGOR

Major Schools:

Colby College
University of New England
University of Maine

Iconic Marks:

Towel Template:

 # MARYLAND

Font Samples and Motifs

State Facts:

baltimore oriole
(state bird)

black-eyed susan
(state flower)

Major Cities:

ANNAPOLIS

BALTIMORE

COLUMBIA

Towel Template:

MARYLAND

Major Schools:

Johns Hopkins University
University of Maryland
United States Naval Academy

Iconic Marks:

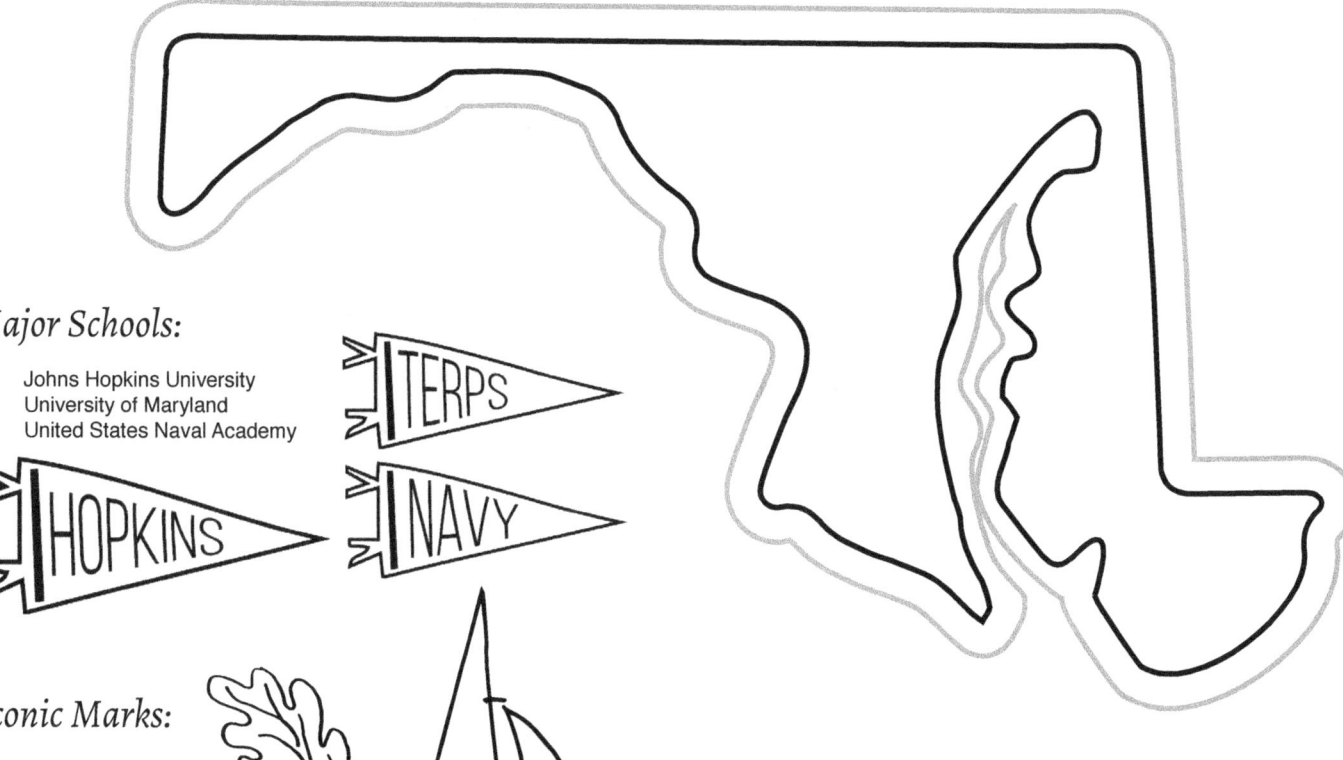

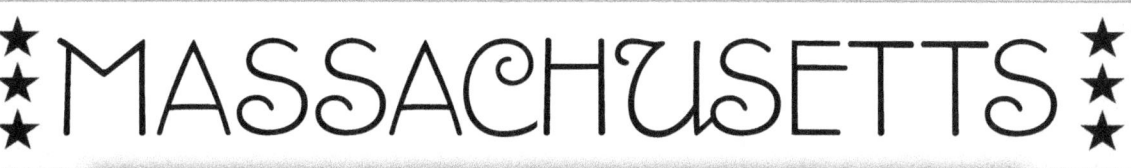

Font Samples and Motifs

State Facts:

black-capped chickadee
(state bird)

mayflower
(state flower)

Major Cities:

BOSTON
WORCESTER
SPRINGFIELD
LOWELL
CAMBRIDGE

Major Schools:

Boston University
University of Massachusetts
Harvard University
Massachusetts Institute of Technology

Iconic Marks:

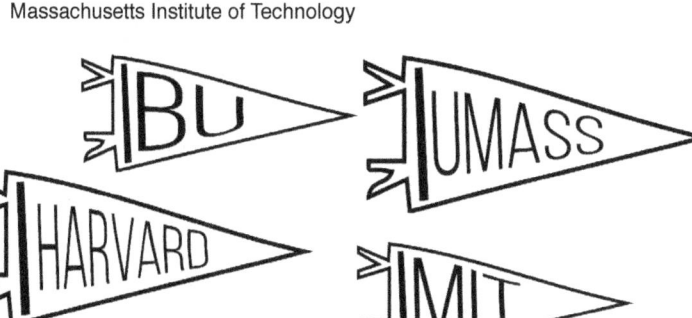

Towel Template:

MASSACHUSETTS

MICHIGAN

Font Samples and Motifs

State Facts:

robin
(state bird)

apple blossom
(state flower)

Major Cities:

LANSING

DETROIT

GRAND RAPIDS

Major Schools:

Michigan State University
University of Michigan
Wayne State University
Central Michigan University

Towel Template:

Iconic Marks:

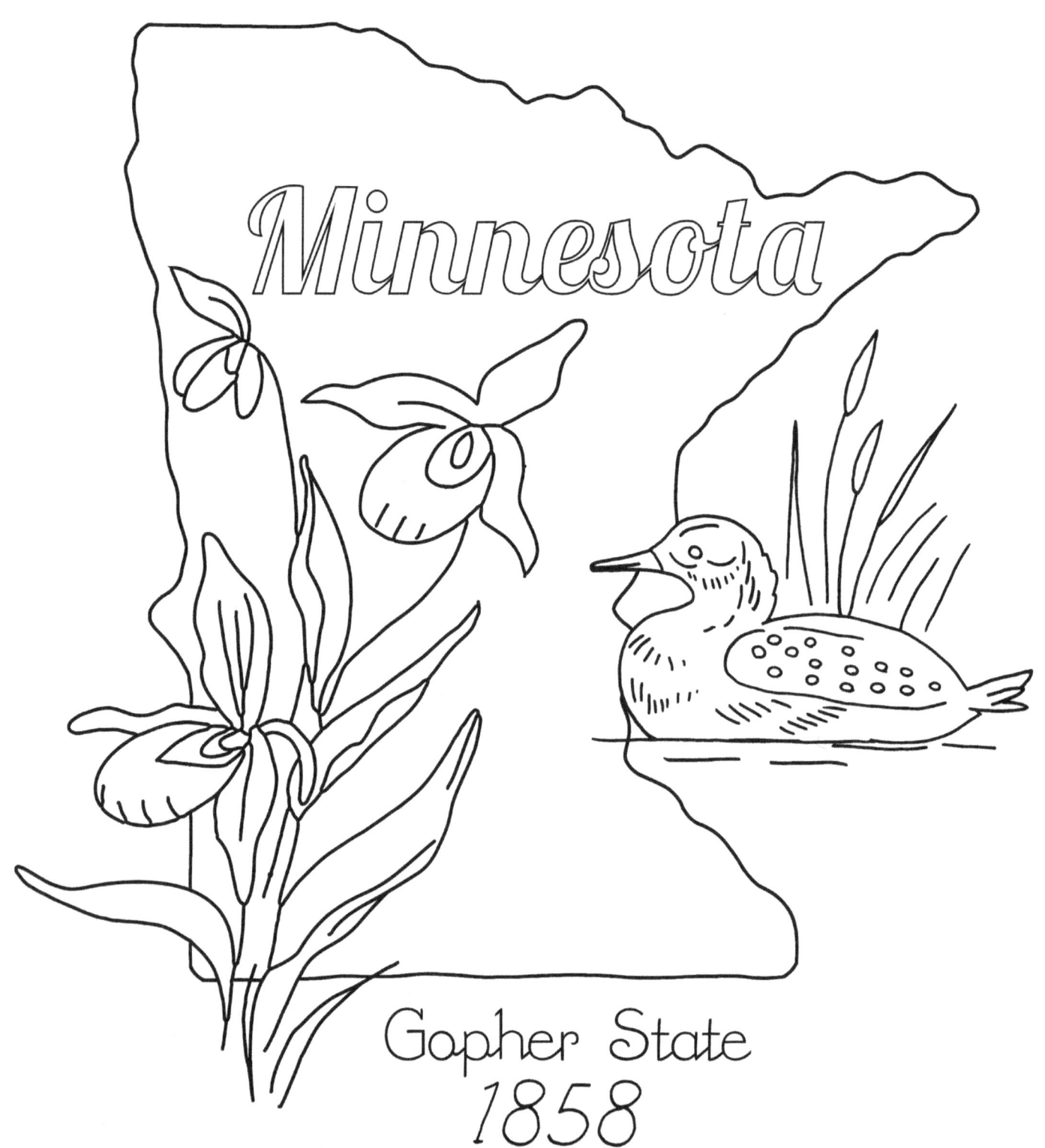

MINNESOTA

Font Samples and Motifs

State Facts:

loon
(state bird)

showy lady's slipper
(state flower)

Major Cities:

SAINT PAUL

MINNEAPOLIS

ROCHESTER

Major Schools:

Minnesota State University
University of Minnesota

Towel Template:

Iconic Marks:

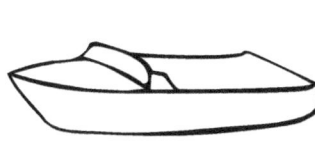

MISSISSIPPI

Font Samples and Motifs

State Facts:

mockingbird
(state bird)

magnolia
(state flower)

Major Cities:

JACKSON
GULFPORT
SOUTHAVEN
BILOXI

Major Schools:

Mississippi State University
University of Mississippi

Towel Template:

Iconic Marks:

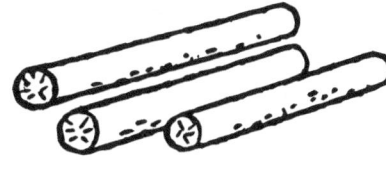

MISSOURI

Font Samples and Motifs

State Facts:

eastern bluebird
(state bird)

hawthorn
(state flower)

♡ ☆

Major Cities:

JEFFERSON CITY
KANSAS CITY
SAINT LOUIS
SPRINGFIELD

Major Schools:

University of Missouri
Saint Louis University
Washington University
Missouri State University

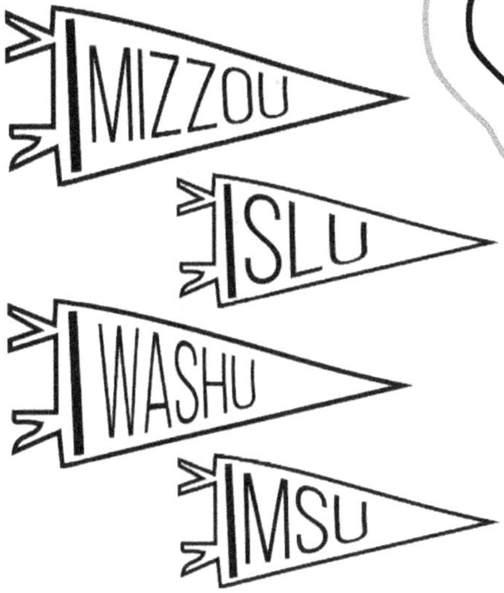

Towel Template:

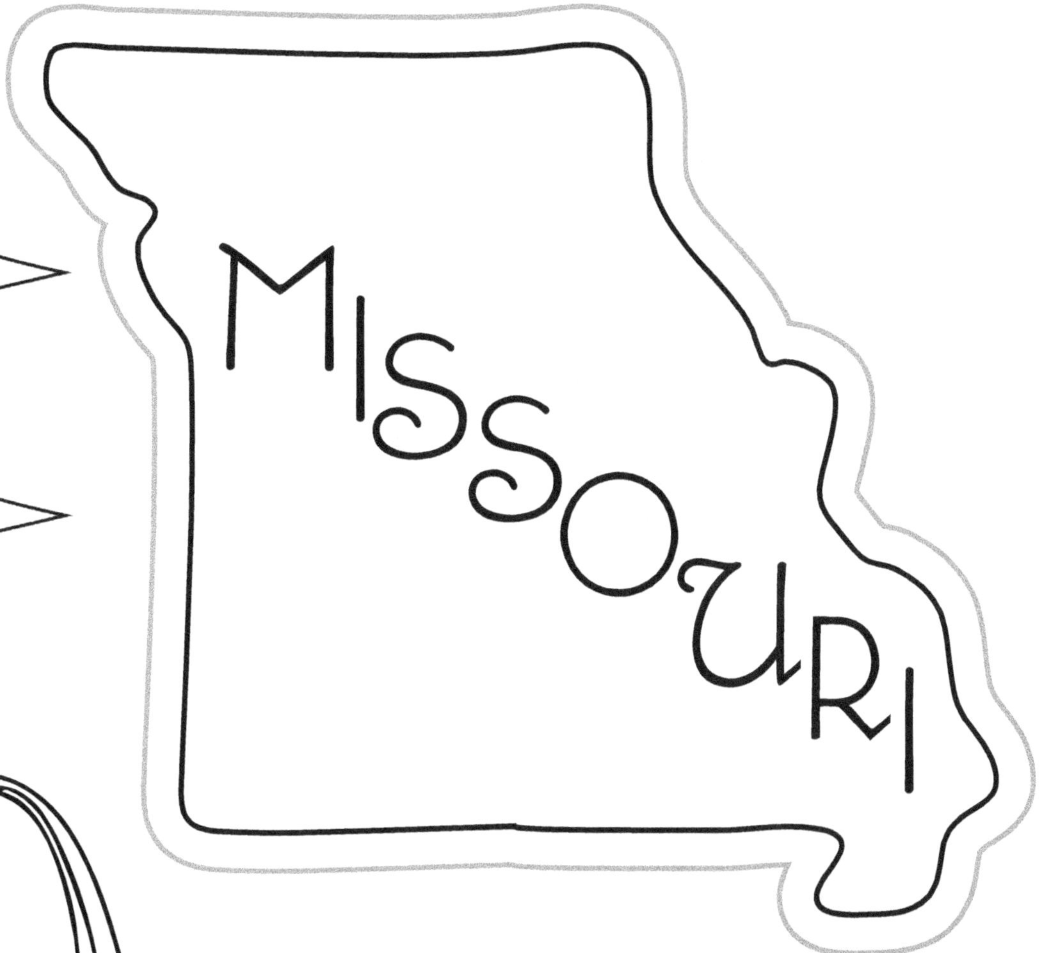

MIZZOU
SLU
WASHU
MSU

Iconic Marks:

ROUTE 66

MISSOURI

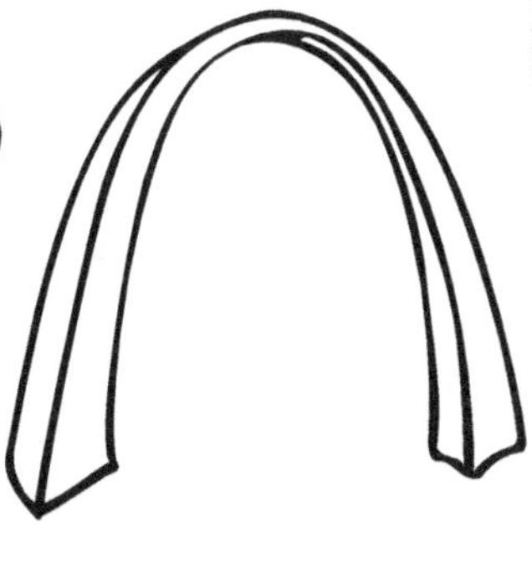

 # MONTANA

Font Samples and Motifs

State Facts:

western meadowlark
(state bird)

bitterroot
(state flower)

Major Cities:

HELENA
BILLINGS
MISSOULA
BOZEMAN

Major Schools:

Montana State University
University of Montana

Iconic Marks:

Towel Template:

NEBRASKA

Font Samples and Motifs

State Facts:

western meadowlark
(state bird)

goldenrod
(state flower)

Major Cities:

LINCOLN

OMAHA

KEARNEY

Major Schools:

Creighton University
University of Nebraska - Lincoln

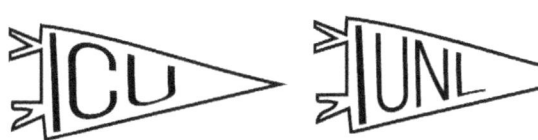

Iconic Marks:

Towel Template:

NEVADA

Font Samples and Motifs

State Facts:

mountain bluebird
(state bird)

sagebrush
(state flower)

Major Cities:

CARSON CITY

LAS VEGAS

RENO

Major Schools:

University of Nevada - Las Vegas
University of Nevada - Reno

Towel Template:

Iconic Marks:

Font Samples and Motifs

State Facts:

purple finch
(state bird)

purple lilac
(state flower)

Major Cities:

CONCORD   EAST CONCORD

MANCHESTER   DERRY VILLAGE

NASHUA

Towel Template:

Major Schools:

Dartmouth College
Plymouth State University
Southern New Hampshire University
University of New Hampshire

Iconic Marks:

NEW HAMPSHIRE

NEW JERSEY

Font Samples and Motifs

State Facts:

goldfinch
(state bird)

purple violet
(state flower)

Major Cities:

TRENTON

NEWARK

JERSEY CITY

Major Schools:

Rutgers, The State University of New Jersey
Princeton University
Seton Hall University

Towel Template:

Iconic Marks:

NEW MEXICO

Font Samples and Motifs

State Facts:

roadrunner
(state bird)

yucca
(state flower)

Major Cities:

SANTA FE

ALBUQUERQUE

LAS CRUCES

Major Schools:

New Mexico State University
University of New Mexico

Iconic Marks:

Towel Template:

NEW YORK

Font Samples and Motifs

State Facts:

eastern bluebird
(state bird)

rose
(state flower)

♡ ☆

Major Cities:

ALBANY MANHATTAN
NEW YORK BRONX
BROOKLYN BUFFALO
QUEENS ROCHESTER

Major Schools:

New York University
Columbia University in the City of New York
Syracuse University
Cornell University

Towel Template:

Iconic Marks:

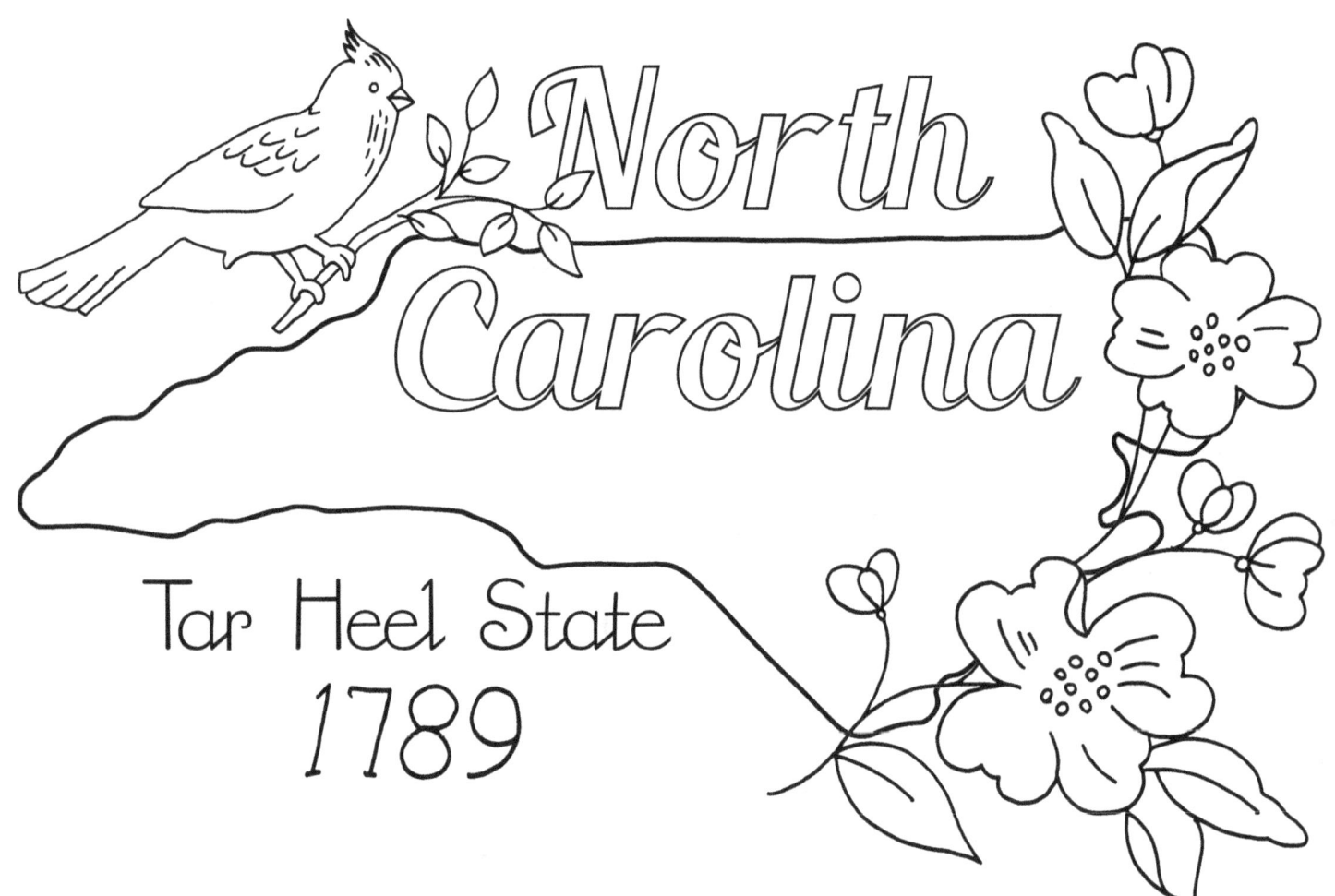

NORTH CAROLINA

Font Samples and Motifs

State Facts:

cardinal
(state bird)

dogwood
(state flower)

Major Cities:

RALEIGH

CHARLOTTE

GREENSBORO

Major Schools:

North Carolina State University
University of North Carolina
Duke University

Iconic Marks:

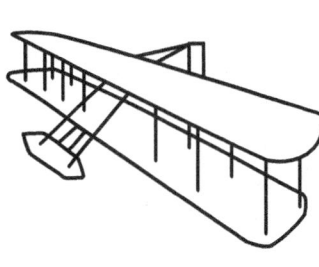

Towel Template:

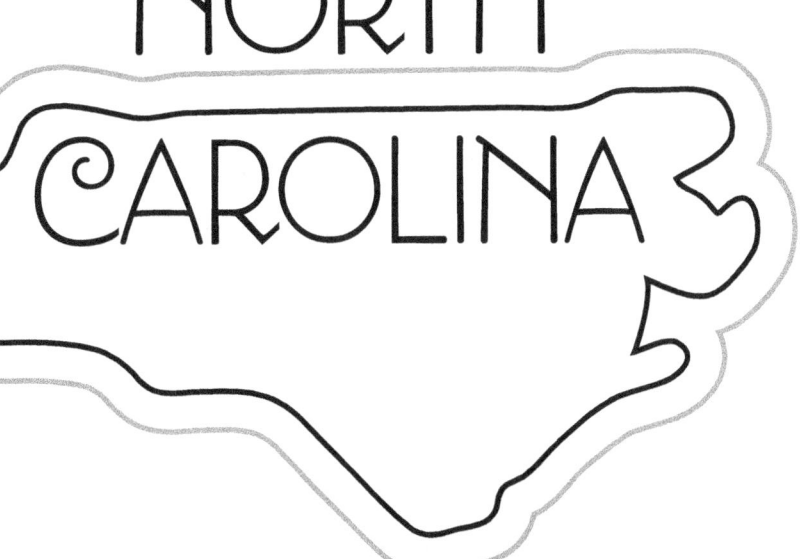

 # NORTH DAKOTA

Font Samples and Motifs

State Facts:

western meadowlark
(state bird)

wild prairie rose
(state flower)

Major Cities:

BISMARK

FARGO

GRAND FORKS

Major Schools:

North Dakota State University
University of North Dakota

Iconic Marks:

Towel Template:

OHIO

Font Samples and Motifs

State Facts:

cardinal
(state bird)

scarlet carnation
(state flower)

♡ ☆

Major Cities:

COLUMBUS

CLEVELAND

CINCINNATI

Major Schools:

Kent State University
Ohio State University
University of Cincinnati
Xavier University

Towel Template:

Iconic Marks:

 # OKLAHOMA

Font Samples and Motifs

State Facts:

scissor-tailed flycatcher
(state bird)

mistletoe
(state flower)

Major Cities:

OKLAHOMA CITY

TULSA

NORMAN

Major Schools:

University of Oklahoma
Oklahoma State University

Iconic Marks:

Towel Template:

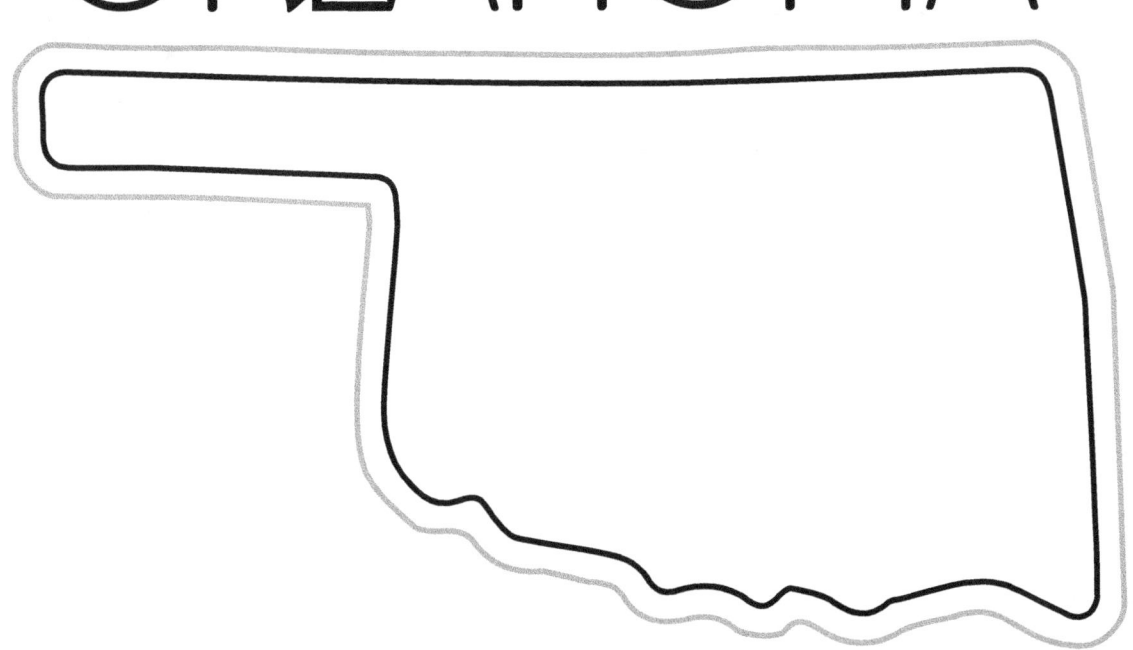

 # OREGON

Font Samples and Motifs

State Facts:

western meadowlark
(state bird)

oregon grape
(state flower)

Major Cities:

SALEM

PORTLAND

EUGENE

Major Schools:

Oregon State University
Portland State University
University of Oregon

Towel Template:

Iconic Marks:

PENNSYLVANIA

Font Samples and Motifs

State Facts:

ruffed grouse
(state bird)

mountain laurel
(state flower)

Major Cities:

HARRISBURG	ALLENTOWN
PHILADELPHIA	ERIE
PITTSBURGH	

Major Schools:

Villanova University
University of Pennsylvania
Pennsylvania State University

Iconic Marks:

Towel Template:

RHODE ISLAND

Font Samples and Motifs

State Facts:

rhode island red
(state bird)

violet
(state flower)

Major Cities:

PROVIDENCE
WARWICK
CRANSTON
PAWTUCKET

Major Schools:

University of Rhode Island
Brown University

Towel Template:

Iconic Marks:

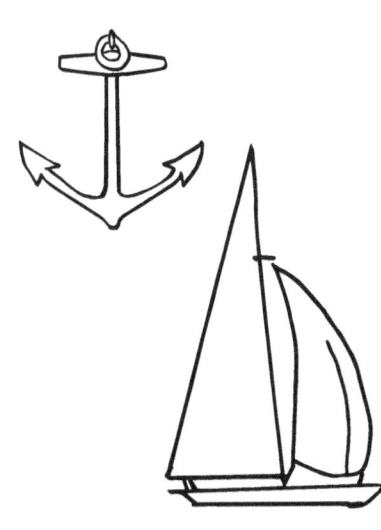

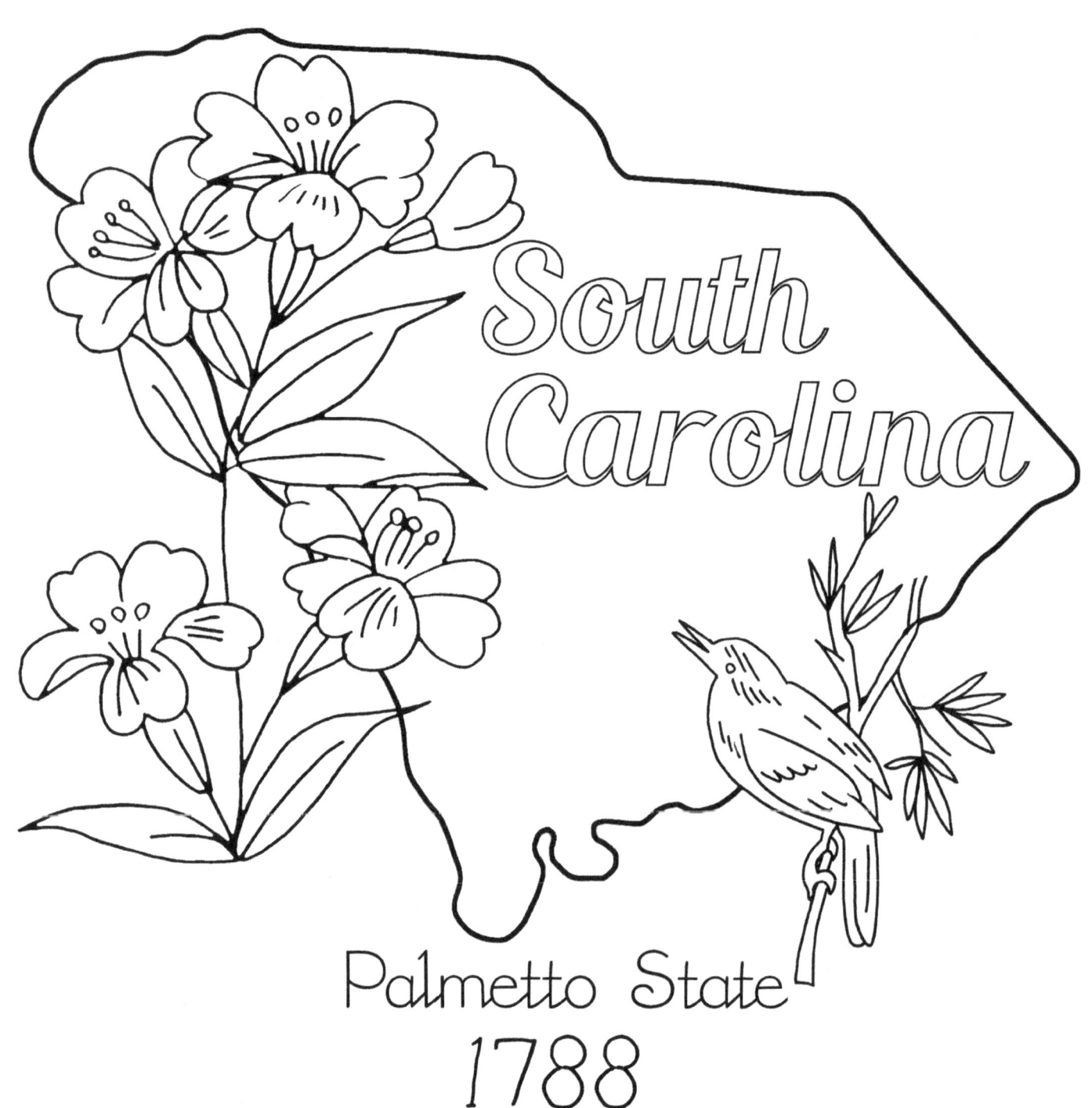

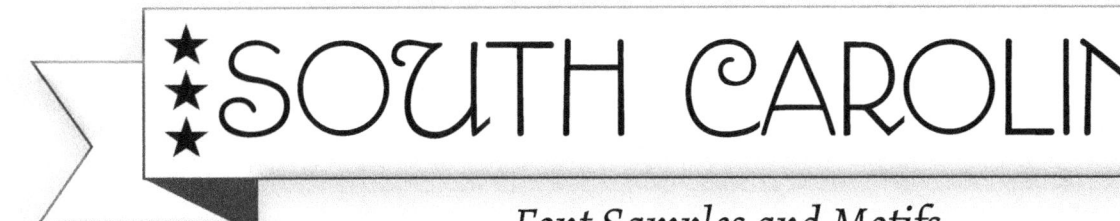

Font Samples and Motifs

State Facts:

carolina wren
(state bird)

yellow jasmine
(state flower)

Major Cities:

COLUMBIA
CHARLESTON
MOUNT PLEASANT
MYRTLE BEACH

Towel Template:

SOUTH CAROLINA

Major Schools:

University of South Carolina
Clemson University

CLEMSON
USC

Iconic Marks:

Font Samples and Motifs

State Facts:

ring-necked pheasant
(state bird)

pasque flower
(state flower)

Major Cities:

PIERRE

SIOUX FALLS

RAPID CITY

Major Schools:

South Dakota State University
University of South Dakota

Iconic Marks:

Towel Template:

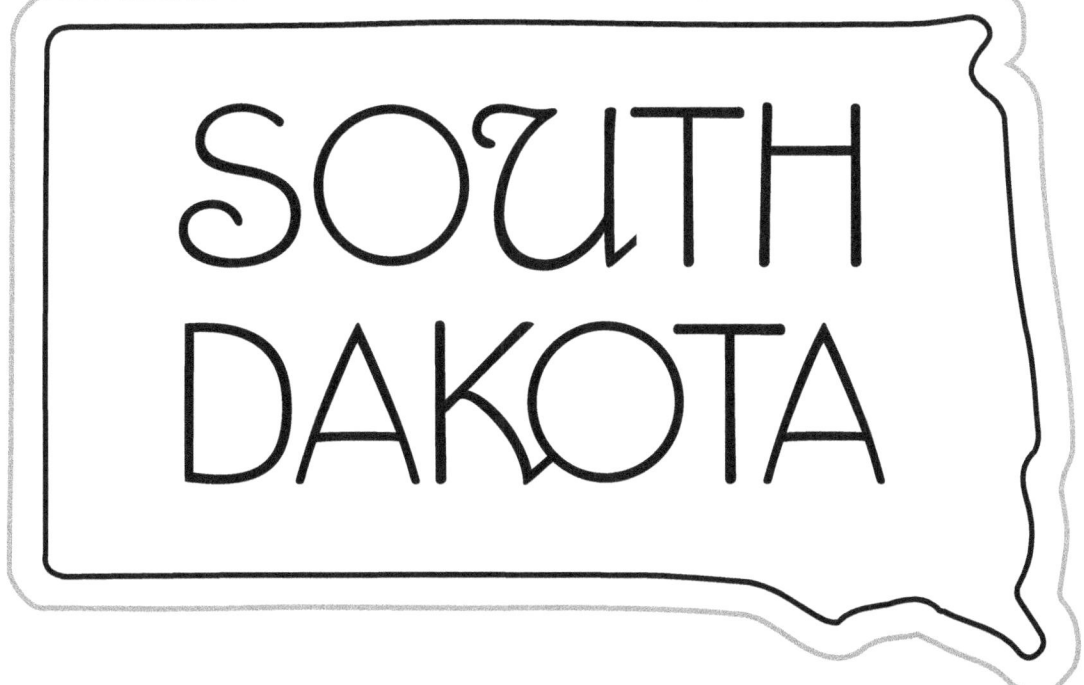

TENNESSEE

Font Samples and Motifs

State Facts:

mockingbird
(state bird)

iris
(state flower)

Major Cities:

NASHVILLE

MEMPHIS

KNOXVILLE

Major Schools:

Vanderbilt University
The University of Tennessee

Iconic Marks:

Towel Template:

 # TEXAS

Font Samples and Motifs

State Facts:

mockingbird
(state bird)

bluebonnet
(state flower)

Major Cities:

AUSTIN   DALLAS

HOUSTON   FORT WORTH

SAN ANTONIO

Major Schools:
Texas A&M University
Rice University
Baylor University
University of Texas

Towel Template:

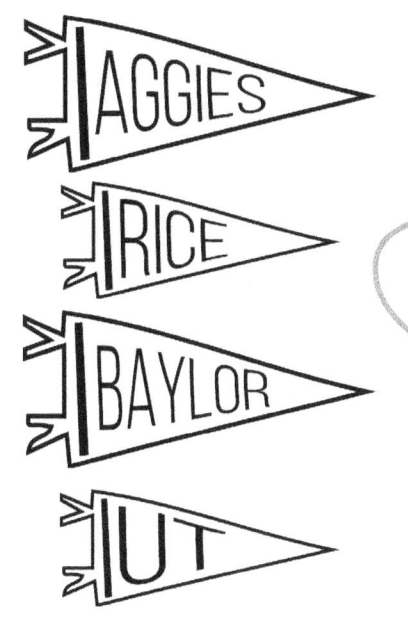

Iconic Marks:

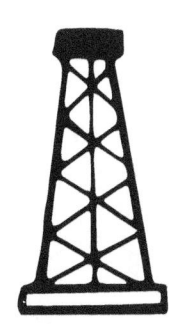  

UTAH

Font Samples and Motifs

State Facts:

california gull
(state bird)

sego lily
(state flower)

♡ ☆

Major Cities:

SALT LAKE CITY

WEST VALLEY CITY

PROVO

Major Schools:

Brigham Young University
Utah State University
University of Utah

Iconic Marks:

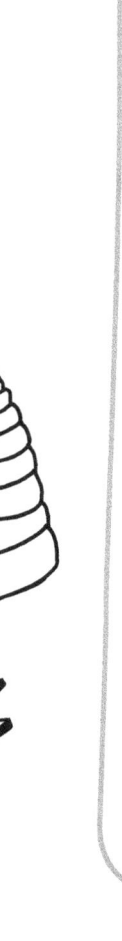

Towel Template:

 # VERMONT

Font Samples and Motifs

State Facts:

hermit thrush
(state bird)

red clover
(state flower)

Major Cities:

MONTPELIER

BURLINGTON

COLCHESTER

Major Schools:

Middlebury College
University of Vermont

Towel Template:

Iconic Marks:

VIRGINIA

Font Samples and Motifs

State Facts:

cardinal
(state bird)

dogwood
(state flower)

Major Cities:

RICHMOND
VIRGINIA BEACH
NORFOLK
ARLINGTON

Major Schools:

George Mason University
Liberty University
University of Virginia
Virginia Commonwealth University

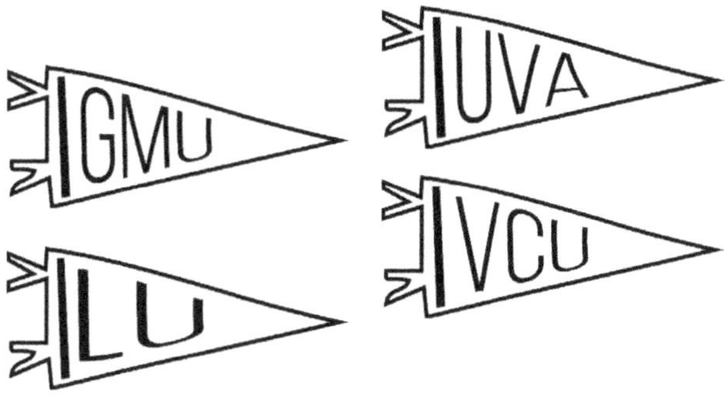

Iconic Marks:

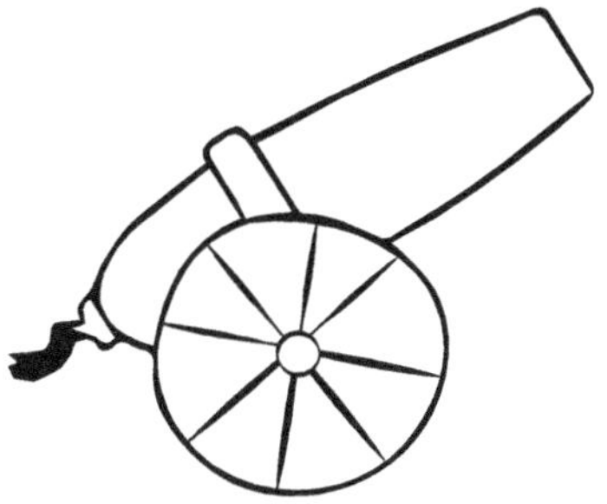

Towel Template:

VIRGINIA

WASHINGTON

Font Samples and Motifs

State Facts:

willow goldfinch
(state bird)

pink rhododendron
(state flower)

Major Cities:

OLYMPIA   TACOMA

SEATTLE   VANCOUVER

SPOKANE

Major Schools:

University of Washington
Washington State University
Gonzaga University

Iconic Marks:

Towel Template:

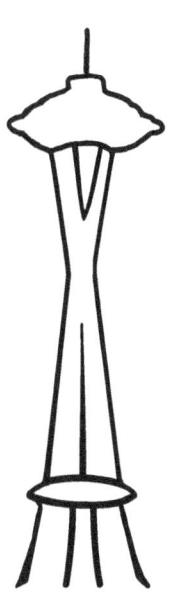

 # WEST VIRGINIA

Font Samples and Motifs

State Facts:

cardinal
(state bird)

pink rhododendron
(state flower)

Major Cities:

CHARLESTON

HUNTINGTON

PARKERSBURG

Major Schools:

Marshall University
West Virginia University

Towel Template:

Iconic Marks:

WISCONSIN

Font Samples and Motifs

State Facts:

robin
(state bird)

violet
(state flower)

♡ ☆

Major Cities:

MADISON

MILWAUKEE

GREEN BAY

Major Schools:

Marquette University
University of Wisconsin - Madison
University of Wisconsin - Milwaukee

Iconic Marks:

Towel Template:

Equality State
1890

WYOMING

Font Samples and Motifs

State Facts:

western meadowlark
(state bird)

indian paintbrush
(state flower)

Major Cities:

CHEYENNE

CASPER

LARAMIE

Major Schools:

University of Wyoming

Iconic Marks:

Towel Template:

Color Key for State Flowers

Apple Blossom
Petals- pale pink; Centers-yellow; Leaves- medium green

Bitterroot
Buds- rose; Petals- pink; Centers- gold; Leaves and Stems- medium green.

Black-Eyed Susan
Petals- yellow; Centers- dark brown; Leaves and Stems- bright green.

Bluebonnet
Flower- purple, blue; Leaves and Stems- grass green.

California Poppy
Petals- orange; Centers- yellow and blue; Leaves & Stems- moss green.

Camelia
Petals- cream; Leaves & Stems- dark green.

Cherokee Rose
Petals- pale pink; Centers- light; Leaves- shades of medium green.

Columbine
Petals- lavender; Centers- pale yellow; Leaves -medium green

Dogwood
Petals- white or pink; Centers- moss green; Stems- brown; Leaves- moss green.

For-Get-Me-Not
Blossoms - Blue; Centers- yellow; leaves-dark green.

Goldenrod
Blossoms- white; Berries- red; Leaves- medium green.

Hawthorn
Blossoms- white; Berries- red; Leaves- medium green.

Hibiscus
Petals- fuchsia; Centers- yellow; Leaves- hunter green.

Indian Paintbrush
Petals- bright red; Leaves and Stems- shades of green.

Iris
Flower- purple or yellow; Buds- deep purple or yellow; Leaves and Stems- dark green.

Magnolia
Petals- white; Centers- yellow; Leaves- medium green.

Mayflower
Blossoms- pale pink; Leaves- medium green.

Mistletoe
Berries- white; Leaves and Stems- moss green.

Mountain Laurel
Buds- rose; Blossoms- pale pink; Leaves & Stems- dark green.

Native Violet
Petals- blue, purple; Centers- light yellow or white; Leaves- hunter green.

Orange Blossom
Petals- white; Centers-orange; Leaves- bright green; Stems- brown.

Oregon Grape
Grape- blue, purple; Leaves- medium green; Outline- red veins.

Pasque Flower
Blossoms- deep lavender; Leaves and Stems- moss green.

Peach Blossom
Petals- rose; Centers- yellow; Buds- deep rose; Leaves and Stems- green.

Peony
Petals- pink, red or white; Center- yellow, Leaves and Stems- dark green.

Pine Cone and Tassel
Cone- rust brown; Needles- hark green; Branches- brown.

Pink Rhododendron
Blossoms- rosy pink; Leaves- dark green.

Purple Lilac
Blossoms- lavender; Leaves and Stems- hunter green.

Purple Violet
Petals- purple; Centers- light yellow or white; Leaves- hunter green.

Red Clover
Clover- shaded red; Leaves and Stems- sea green.

Rose
Flower- shades of dark red; Leaves and Stems- emerald green.

Sagebrush
Dots- gold; Leaves and Stems- jade green.

Saguaro Cactus
Petals- white; Center-tan with white sprout; Stalk & Bud-green; Single lines below- rust

Scarlet Carnation
Buds and Flowers- dark red; Leaves- medium green.

Sego Lily
Petals- white; Centers- orange; Leaves and Stems- green.

Showy Lady's Slipper
Top of Flower- white; Bottom- pink; Leaves- dark green.

Sunflower
Petals- deep yellow; Center- brown; Leaves and Stems- moss green.

Syringa
Petals- very light blue (almost white); Centers- yellow; Leaves and Stems- dark green.

Wild Prairie Rose
Petals- pale pink; Centers- light; Leaves- shades of medium green.

Wild Rose
Petals- pale pink; Centers- light; Leaves- shades of medium green.

Violet
Petals- blue, purple; Centers- light yellow or white; Leaves- hunter green.

Yellow Jasmine
Blossoms- deep yellow; Leaves- apple green.

Yucca
Flowers- beige; Leaves- shades of green.

Color Key for State Birds

Baltimore Oriole
Body- black with orange patch in center of top of Tail and orange Breast; Feet- brown.

Black-capped Chickadee
Body, Tail, Wings- gray with touches of black and white at end of Wings; rest of Body- lighter gray to white; Head- white with black cap; Patch under Throat- white; Beak and Feet- black.

Blue Hen Chicken
Actually an historic name for some soldiers of Delaware – so the hen should be done in Blue.

Brown Pelican
Back, Tail- dark to grayish brown; Wings, Head, Chest, Side of Neck- tan; Edges of Pouch- white.

Brown Thrasher
Top of Head- Back, Wings and Tail- chestnut brown; Spots on Breast- dark brown; Beak- gray; Feet- brown.

Cactus Wren
Crown, Back of Neck- brown; Body- dark brown; Rump- grayish brown; Tail- black; over Eye- white; under Eye brown stripe; Iris- red.

California Gull
Body- white; Back, Wings- blue-gray; Long Wing Feathers- black with white markings; Bill- yellow (red spot on lower Bill, Black on upper); Legs- blue; Webs- yellow.

California Quail
Body- brown with white spots; Feathers- edges in black; white stripe above Eye, continuing down Neck and circling above Breast under Beak; Breast- slate blue; Legs- brown.

Cardinal
Body- Cardinal red with touch of black around Beak; Beak and Feet- red.

Carolina Wren
Bird- rust brown; Wings and Tail- dull brown; Rum and upper Tail- light chestnut.

Eastern Bluebird
Head, Back, Wings and Tail- dull brown; Rump and upper Tail- light chestnut.

Flicker
Back, Breast-tan and black; Top of Head- blue-gray, with a red patch at back of Neck; Eye, Beak, Patch under Eye, Tail- black; Feet- gray.

Goldfinch
Body, Beak- yellow; Forehead; Black; Wings, Tail- black with white; Feet- brown.

Hermit Thrush
Body- gray brown; Tail- red-brown; tail- red-brown; Beak- black; Feet- flesh colored.

Lark Bunting
Body- gray with white patch on Wings; Beak- gray; Feet- yellow.

Loon
Body- black with white spots; Neck- greenish purple; bill- gray.

Mockingbird
Bird- gray; Wings, tail, Beak and feet- darker gray.

Mountain Bluebird
Head, Back, Wings and Tail- medium blue with black along tips of Wings; Throat, Breast- chestnut brown; Beak and Feet- black.

Nene Goose
Entire bird- shaded light and medium grays.

Purple Finch
Bird- wine purple; Wings and Tails- brownish red; Abdomen- white.

Ptarmigan
Body- medium chestnut brown with white; Crown- deep brown.

Ring-necked Pheasant
Body- copper brown with green, blue black, buff and purple markings, neck- white ring up to top of Head with dark green and blue (colors seem metallic).

Rhode Island Red
Body, Plumage- red brown; Legs- yellow or red.

Roadrunner
Bird- glossy olive green; Tips of Feathers- white.

Robin
Head- Wings, Tail- dark brown; Back- medium brown; Breast- orange, than or red; Beak and Feet- yellow.

Ruffed Grouse
Bird- shaded medium and dark browns; Beak and Feet- dark brown.

Scissor-tailed Flycatcher
Head, Back- gray; Breast, Underbody- white; Sides of Body- salmon; Base of Crown Feathers- white.

Western Meadowlark
Back of Body; Wings, Tail- speckled with brown; Head, Patches near Eyes, some Feathers in Tail- white; Underbody- yellow.

Willow Goldfinch
Body, Beak- yellow; Forehead- black; Wings, Tail- black with white; Feet- brown.

Lettering Alphabet

ABCDEFGHIJKLM
NOPQRSTUVWXYZ
1234567890
abcdefghijklmnopqrstuvwxyz

ABCDEFGHIJKLMNOPQRSTU
VWXYZ 1234567890
abcdefghijklmnopqrstuvwxyz

ABCDEFGHIJKLMNOPQRSTUVWXYZ
1234567890

abcdefghijklmnopqrstuvwxyz
1234567890

Thank you for purchasing *Land That I Love!* All my life I have been fascinated by fashion, sewing and all things vintage. As the owner of Indygo Junction, a sewing pattern company, and author of a library of craft books, I have been inspired by needle arts publications that have been published throughout the years. Here are just a few of our embroidery releases from IndygoJunction.com:

If you enjoyed this book and share my passion for vintage, visit AmyBarickman.com for more of my collection of curated content including books for needle and thread, inspiring fabrics and textiles, as well as many more publications including my book *Vintage Notions: An Inspirational Guide to Needlework, Sewing, Cooking, Fashion & Fun* as well as the companion magazine *Vintage Notions Monthly*.

www.amybarickman.com
Find free images, inspiration and books for the sewing and needle arts!

www.indygojunction.com
Featuring digital & print patterns, books, tutorials, giveaways, project ideas, & more!

Subscribe to each of our eNewsletters to learn about new products, receive special offers, discounts, videos, and get a FREE eBook!

www.ingramcontent.com/pod-product-compliance
Lightning Source LLC
Chambersburg PA
CBHW081005180426
43194CB00044B/2815